Ella

A LIFE UNABORTED

JENNIFER WILKINS

WESTBOW
PRESS
A DIVISION OF THOMAS NELSON

WestBow Press books may be ordered through booksellers or by contacting:

WestBow Press
A Division of Thomas Nelson
1663 Liberty Drive
Bloomington, IN 47403
www.westbowpress.com
1-(866) 928-1240

Because of the dynamic nature of the Internet, any web addresses or links contained in this book may have changed since publication and may no longer be valid. The views expressed in this work are solely those of the author and do not necessarily reflect the views of the publisher, and the publisher hereby disclaims any responsibility for them.

Any people depicted in stock imagery provided by Thinkstock are models, and such images are being used for illustrative purposes only.

Certain stock imagery © Thinkstock.

ISBN: 978-1-4497-2893-9 (sc)

Library of Congress Control Number: 2011918768

Printed in the United States of America

WestBow Press rev. date: 10/18/2011

To Rev. Robert Miller, my grandfather; AKA "Grandpa Bob", the man that taught me what it truly means to live for Jesus:Thank you for choosing to live for Jesus instead of self, for looking to Him in every circumstance, and sharing Him with others no matter the consequence. I am blessed to have witnessed a true relationship between man and God! One day, you will hear the words of your best friend saying,"Well done, good and faithful servant"!

"No eye has seen, no ear has heard, no mind has conceived what God has prepared for those who love Him."

❧ 1 Corinthians 2:9

CONTENTS

List of Illustrations

Photo of newborn Ella

Photo of Jen holding Ella

Photo of Ella on CPAP

Photo of Ella the night she was anointed

Photo of Ella with her eye bandages

Photo of Ella in her harness

Photo of Ella in her first cast

Photo of Ella in Peru

Photo of Ella in her wheelchair

Photo of Ella and her sister, Ariana

Preface

I have to tell my story for fear that if I do not, my heart and mind will explode. I have felt led to share the deepest parts of my journey with others so that if they too are going through a rough patch, a tragic loss, or even if they're in the midst of life's blessings, maybe my story can touch them in some way. I have said ever since I was a kid that if God hasn't taken us right up to heaven after we're "saved," there must be a reason that He has us on this earth; I believe it's so that we can lead others to Him. That is the one and only reason I can logically think of that God would leave us here in this harsh world and not take us up to be in His awesome presence.

So, I am here to share my story in hopes that others can see God through my eyes and meet the Savior I know, and in doing so, commit their lives to Him so that they can experience the peace and joy that only He can bring. Because if I'm not in heaven, my purpose is to share Jesus with every person I come in contact with so that they can walk with Him as I have. So that they can weep with Him as I have. And so that they can experience His miracles, just as I have.

What I am about to tell you is no ordinary story. It will be from my perspective, but it is all true. If I can ask you to do anything while you're reading this book, it's to believe it. My hope is that you will be able to feel what I felt, jump into my shoes, and experience God like never before.

Acknowledgments

I am always amazed at the way in which God works. At a young age, I enjoyed writing short stories and telling tales, but never did I imagine that God would give me a story like this to introduce to paper. I feel completely inadequate to have been given this amazing opportunity to be used by our King of Kings and Lord of Lords, Jesus Christ! And because I am sufficiently insufficient, I have many to thank for making this book a possibility!

Never will I fully understand why God chose to allow me this life-changing experience, but I will forever be grateful for this chance to serve Him. My first "thank you" goes to Him, my Jesus, because when He looked at me and pondered what He should do with my life, He did not see the mess of a person that I was, but instead saw His precious child, whom He loved dearly. Jesus saved me from the lake of fire and eternal suffering and gave me instead an amazing opportunity to serve Him, the Creator of our universe, and to bask in the presence of the Almighty God for all of eternity! I cannot imagine a more abundantly satisfying destiny, and it's only because of the grace of Jesus Christ. To Him be all the glory! Thank you Jesus!

Secondly, this story would not exist without the diligence and hard work it took my parents to raise me up in faith. From a young age, I was taught the importance of following Jesus and how committing all that I am to God would not always be the easy path, but would be the one that held the greatest reward. I owe my worldview and my sturdy faith in

1

The Beginning of the End

IT HAPPENED ON FRIDAY, FEBRUARY 15, 2008. I woke up at 10:00 p.m. soaking wet! I could tell that it wasn't sweat because it wasn't all over. It wasn't urine, or at least I hoped it wasn't; how embarrassing to try and explain to my husband, Calvin, that I had wet the bed! Just to make sure, I smelled it, but there was no odor. Could I have wet the bed as an adult? What other possibility was there? I was pregnant, but wasn't due until July 17! Could my water have broken five months early? Was it possible? There was no blood. Just water. I got out of bed, grabbed my cell phone from the floor and quietly walked into the bathroom that was connected to our bedroom. After inspecting my wet clothing more closely and realizing that I was still "leaking," I suspected that it was indeed my water that had broken. I moved farther through my bathroom and into our adjacent closet, closed the door, and began changing out of my wet night clothes.

I debated whether or not to wake up Cal, but my mind "logically" told me that there was nothing we could do if it was my water that had broken, so I let him sleep. I decided that I would wake him up if I needed to go to the doctor.

After I changed and applied a pad (because I was still leaking fluid), I called my doctor's after-hours number just to find out if there was anything in particular I should be doing. With amniotic fluid streaming steadily out of my body, I knew that my baby would die, but I wasn't sure what the standard procedure was in these situations. Since I was 18 weeks pregnant

1

, farther along than when most miscarriages take place, I wasn't sure if there was anything special that needed to be done.

I dialed the after-hours number only to get an answering service that told me to wait for the doctor to call within 20 minutes. I waited in my closet, the one place that would keep me from disturbing Cal or Ariana, my one-and-a-half-year-old daughter who was asleep in her bedroom. With my back against the inside of our closet door, I slowly lowered myself down to the floor as my mind began to race and analyze what had just happened.

About six months prior to this, I had experienced a miscarriage. One of the hardest parts about it had been going through those first several weeks of pregnancy only to end up with no baby. Morning sickness has always been very present with each of my pregnancies, so to go through eight weeks of pure exhaustion, throwing up and in a zombie-like state, only to end up with no reward and a bruised heart, had seemed like a grand waste of time. The miscarriage took its toll on me, but the emotional effects had not been unbearable because I had my sweet Ariana to love on and snuggle.

Now, as I sat on my closet floor, waiting for the call from my doctor, thoughts of my miscarriage attacked my heart like a swarm of ants on a tasty picnic. My mind automatically started blaming God. I started screaming in my head, "God, why would you let this happen *again*? Only this time, I've felt my baby move! This time, my belly is starting to show, this time we waited to tell everyone that we were pregnant until the second trimester safety zone, and now . . . *now* . . . I don't know. If you don't want me to have any more kids, why do you let me get pregnant? Should I just stop trying? I'm not one of those ladies who can emotionally or physically handle being pregnant several times and having them all result in miscarriage. I'm just not. I just can't. What are your plans for me Lord?" Emotions of anger, bitterness, and deep unexplainable sorrow surged through my veins as I silently cried out to the Lord.

" *Have Peace.*" I felt the words resound in my heart. Was it God? Was He talking to me? Suddenly my mind stilled and I listened. *"Have Peace,"* He said again. It *was* God! No, He wasn't speaking audibly, but it was a sensation that I cannot explain. I knew that it was Him talking to me—I wasn't sure how, but He was! It was as if His amazing love was wrapping tightly around me and assuring me that it was all going to be OK. His peace rushed in and filled my heart, leaving no corner untouched. God's undeniable presence filled my closet and He began to work in me.

I was suddenly reminded of a time in my life, only one year prior, when I had been struggling with the idea of being a mother after Ariana was born. Before her birth, I had worked for my dad in his glass shop as a receptionist and had constantly been in contact with people. My love for the Lord had always been strong, and I considered myself more outgoing about sharing the love of Jesus with others than most young people my age; my job was my area of impact.

One summer, there was a girl who worked in the snow-cone shack on the edge of my dad's company lot. Her name was Jessie. After talking with her almost every day, a friendship sprouted. Occasionally, I shared with her about Jesus and how much He loved her. One day, after inviting her to my youth group, she agreed to come with me. Jessie's first visit to our youth group was a huge success and she started becoming more involved. When she had been attending church with me for a few months, we both went on the senior high winter retreat with my youth group, where Jessie accepted Christ as her personal Savior and allowed Him to change her life. It was situations and opportunities like this that gave purpose to my life, and so I thought that being a stay-at-home mom was taking away my opportunity to share Jesus Christ with others. Don't get me wrong. I *loved* staying at home with my little Ariana. She was my little mini-me, we were attached all the time, but staying at home gave me a sense of frustration because I did not feel like I was ministering as I had before.

It was during that time that I frequently prayed that God would send people for me to talk with, to share His love with, and to pray with whenever I was out and about. I remembered praying that God would cause me to bump into people who needed His love, and if I wasn't out of the house for a day or two, I'd pray that He'd send a sales person or a neighbor to my house so that I could minister even as a stay-at-home mom.

God caused me to remember this prayer and the desire of my heart to tell others about Him as I sat waiting for the phone call from my doctor. Alone within the four walls of my closet, I felt God speak to my heart again, but this time it was a question:"*Jen, are you still willing to minister in any situation that comes your way?*" It came abruptly. I hadn't been ready for the question. I knew exactly what He was asking. God wanted to know if I was willing to be used in this devastating situation with the possibility of *another* miscarriage! The question represented a choice for me to let go of my situation and give it to God or to hold on and cling to my own devices to get me through. Letting go would free myself from self-pity and bitterness, but it also would leave me vulnerable to whatever God had for me. Had God allowed this situation to happen to answer my prayers to witness to people?

I knew my baby was going to die. That much was certain. I also knew that it was not God that caused it to happen.

I closed my eyes, took a deep breath, and answered, "Yes, Lord, with all my heart I want to minister and serve you." And His reply blazed into my heart as a burning motivator, "*This is your chance. This situation has the power to break and destroy you, or you can give it to me and I will use it to create something beautiful.*" I knew what my answer was, but my throat was so thick, it was hard to answer. So it came out in a whisper, "OK, God, use it." The words were painful, like admitting that my baby was going to die.

As I relinquished any and all control from the situation, at that moment God filled me with a supernatural understanding that everything was going to be OK. An absolute peace covered my entire being. I'm not sure how to explain it except to say that I was no longer sick to my stomach, I wasn't angry, just tranquil and at complete ease with my circumstances. I knew that my baby was going to die, but she would die whether I gave this situation to God or not. In my 23 years of life experience, I had already learned that God did not cause bad things to happen, but He could use them to bring about good. If God could be glorified by my baby's death and by the peace that surrounded me, then let it be so. I knew that I would see my baby again one day. She was going to the place I wanted to be, the only perfect place there is: Heaven!

By letting go, I was free. The bitterness and anger couldn't touch me. The situation was God's. It had been His anyway. What if I had held on? What if I had fought for a life that was going to end and then been bitter that my baby died? That would have destroyed me. I feel that God gave me the insight to see ahead of time what "holding on" would do to me and allowed me to see the beauty of the situation. It was as if my closet was the cocoon of a growing caterpillar, and right there, in that closet, I was transformed into a butterfly. I went in as a baby in understanding and was made into a new creature. It was as if my eyes were open and I could see the situation from God's perspective. These next words are going to sound strange, but it's exactly how I felt. The emotion of *excitement* flooded my heart and entire being. I could not *wait* to see what God was going to do. A promise from the Almighty had just been given to me that He was going to use *me* to bring others to Him through my little baby!

Just then, my phone rang. I took a deep breath and answered to the voice of my doctor, Julene Hicks. It was too far-fetched for her to believe that my water had broken at only 18 weeks of pregnancy, but since I was still leaking some sort of fluid, she wanted to check me for infection and to see how the baby was doing. She directed me to go to the Labor and Delivery unit in the hospital instead of the Emergency Room so that I could get immediate care and told me that she'd meet me there in 20 minutes. When we hung up, I decided it was time to wake up Calvin.

Once I explained the situation to Cal, he wanted to take me to the hospital, but in order for him to do that, we'd have to wake up our daughter, Ari, and take her with us, or wait for someone to come over and stay with her. Neither option was ideal, and considering that I needed to get to the hospital as soon as possible, I opted to go alone while Cal called to get someone to stay with Ari so he could join me later.

On the way to the hospital a cloud of thoughts consumed me once again. One interesting idea that crept into my mind was the possibility that my baby could still be alive. I had just assumed that my baby was probably already dead, because my pregnancy was terminating itself. That assumption probably came from comparing this pregnancy with my miscarriage. But the concept that she could still be alive at that moment was very odd and gave me a sense of urgency to get to the hospital before all the fluid leaked out.

With this new need to rush came an onslaught of "road blocks." In our small town of Nampa, Idaho, I hadn't anticipated anything hindering my drive. It was close to midnight, you'd think that the roads would be empty; but no, it was me . . . and a grandma. She was driving *so* slowly. I remember talking to her in my mind, saying things like, "Aren't you supposed to be in bed?" or "Could you go any slower?" But I was reminded once again that God was in control, and He knew that this little old lady was going to be in front of me on the way to the hospital. If He wanted my baby to live, He wouldn't let her die.

With that realization, I calmed some, until I felt more fluid rush out! It was time for my newfound calm to be tested. And to add to the pressure and frustration, the safety gates were coming down at the upcoming railroad crossing! "Sure!" I thought, "A grandma *and* a train all on the same night!" So, what was usually a 15-minute trip became a 30-minute trip.

Once I arrived safely at our local hospital, I was immediately taken to a bed that they had waiting for me between two hanging curtains with beds on either side. As a nurse proceeded to hook me up to an IV, I told her that it has always been hard for nurses to start IVs on me, and that the vein in the bend of my arm was her best bet. She wanted to follow protocol, however, and start from the hand. So, I endured as she poked me over and over and twisted all around trying to get that silly needle into the correct spot. Finally, after what seemed like five minutes of pressing, twisting, and bending beneath my skin, the nurse decided that my hand was not a good spot. "Hmmm, ya *think*!" I screamed in my mind.

All I wanted was Calvin. It would have been so much easier if he were there with me. But even as these human thoughts were flooding to the surface, God was whispering to my heart, "*Be calm.*" Another time I felt Him say, "*I'm here. Remember, I'll get you through.*" And I was flooded with the peace that only comes from above and reminded that this was not about my pain, frustration, or emotional grief, but about giving every second to my Lord and Savior, Jesus Christ. Hopefully as I did so, others would be able to see that there was someone bigger getting me through.

After the nurse had tried every spot imaginable in my arm *except* for the spot I told her would work, she finally conceded and tried the vein in the bend of my arm. It was a hit! Luckily, I hadn't said anything rude to her during the whole ordeal, just smiled and said, "It's OK, we'll just try again," as my eyes were watering from the sting and ache. Now, if that wasn't God helping me to control my tongue, I don't know what it was, because the words were sure flying in my mind.

Once I was successfully hooked up to the IV fluids, my doctor came in. I'll never forget the look on her face. Normally, Dr. Hicks was the image of happiness, words bubbling out with excitement, but in this moment her face was completely blank, almost nervous. The nurses had checked the fluid I was leaking and it tested positive for being amniotic fluid, which meant my water *had* broken, and it was only a matter of time until it was all gone.

The words Dr. Hicks spoke next caught me off guard. "I can't believe this has happened," she said with the most defeated eyes, "It only happens to about one percent of pregnant women. I've never had a patient experience this before now." Dr. Hicks was the most amazing doctor I had ever met. So caring, so wise, she only divulged information to her pregnant patients that would not make them stress or wonder needlessly about the wellbeing of their babies, and she always made the process very exciting. My favorite aspect about her was that she was a Christian.

I remember her telling me that she would often bring teen moms into her clinic to give them free ultrasounds so that they'd re-think abortion and consider adopting out their babies. She had a way with people and displayed Christ's love in everything she did. But as I looked at her now, the energy and spunk that she normally displayed were completely gone, and in their place was a look of devastation.

I could tell by the look in her eyes that this situation was close to her heart. We shared an eternal bond in Jesus Christ, and because it wasn't a situation that she had ever dealt with before, I think it heightened her sense of awareness and made her want to perform at the top of her game.

"So, what do we do now?" I asked. I could see the wheels of her mind turning, and after a brief pause it seemed that she suddenly remembered a helpful piece of information, "We'll do an ultrasound to see the status of your baby, and then maybe we can try a few days of bed rest to see if the sac will reseal itself. In some cases," she added, "The sacs have resealed and filled back up with fluid, and the babies have survived. But it only works in *some* cases. About one in ten sacs will reseal." The odds were not promising at all, but before I had time to process any more, Dr. Hicks continued,

"First, let's do an ultrasound and see how the baby's doing, and then we can make a plan of action based on what we find."

I was moved from the bed between curtains to an actual hospital room. As I waited for the ultrasound machine to come, I wondered when Calvin would arrive. I had sure been lonely without him and had already been at the hospital an hour by the time the machine arrived. When the gel was squeezed out onto my tummy, my heart began to race. What were they going to find? Would my baby be dead? Would it be alive? I inhaled deep breaths into my lungs and tried to once again hand the situation over to Jesus. "Take my worry, Lord. Make me free from this anxiety," I prayed earnestly. And again, His peace rushed in and set my whole body at ease.

My doctor placed the monitor onto my stomach, and in that instant my heart dropped. We didn't hear anything.

2

Wading through the Fog

THEN, A MOMENT LATER, IT CAME. A heartbeat, fast and steady, rang out through the speakers of the ultrasound machine. My own heart skipped a beat at the knowledge that right then, at that very moment, my little child was still alive! This brought all sorts of possibilities to the table, and I was determined to lie as still as possible so as to help that sac reseal and create a comfy home for our little babe.

The next task for the ultrasound tech was to measure the fluid that still remained in my amniotic sac. "Six centimeters," my doctor whispered, "You've already lost quite a bit of fluid, but we'll see if lying still and reclining your bed to help gravity keep the fluid in helps to reseal the sac." "What level of fluid does a normal womb have and how long does it normally take to heal?" I asked with a straight face, bracing myself for bad news.

"A typical womb has anywhere from 10 to 20 centimeters, and we usually give this treatment one or two days to work." She continued, "Sometimes it will heal quickly; other times, it will not heal at all, but two days is the maximum because we are running a risk of infection with your womb being open to bacteria right now. We've given you some antibiotics to cover you for these next few days." I took a deep breath and geared up to lay flat for the next two days. I'd try anything to get this little baby here safely.

After the initial points of interest had been reviewed with the ultrasound, I had a request of my own. "Since we couldn't tell a gender last week at my appointment, would you mind looking this time?" Had I known what a difficult task I had just requested, I probably would not have asked. Because of the lower fluid levels, the baby was squished, which made it much more difficult to discern a gender. Dr. Hicks gave it her best shot, "Well, if I had to guess, I'd say . . . girl." I could tell it was a shot in the dark, but I appreciated it. "A girl," I thought. "Well, that will be easy; we already have one girl, so I could reuse everything if my sac does decide to heal up and give this little baby a chance at life."

....

For a few moments, I was alone, and it dawned on me that I should probably let my parents know that I was in the hospital. They were in McCall, Idaho, a city in the mountains, on a winter retreat with our church's youth group. My youngest sister, Monica, who was a sophomore in high school, was on the trip, and my parents were very involved in helping out wherever they could.

The phone was ringing . . . my dad answered. "Hey, Dad?" "Yeah?" Because it was late, and I could tell by the sound of his voice that he had been sleeping, I began rattling off my purpose for the call: "I'm in the hospital because my water broke. I'm OK, but they're going to keep me in here to try and see if my sac will seal shut and give the baby a chance to make it. It's a very, very small chance that the baby could make it, but will you pray that God would give me the grace and peace I need so that the nurses and doctors would be able to see Jesus in me?" There was silence on the other end for a moment and then, with a mixture of sleepiness and disappointment, my dad answered, "I'm so sorry, Jen. We'll be praying, honey." "Thanks, Dad."

As I hung up the phone, I felt a surge of adrenaline that brought forth strength that I hadn't felt before. A thought occurred to me—I needed prayer, and lots of it! I had to call Grandpa. My grandfather was a pastor at our church. Not the senior pastor, but he had the title of Pastoral Care, which basically means that he cared for the people of the church and community. For years he had made hospital visits, officiated weddings and funerals, and stopped in just to check on people. My grandpa, Rev. Robert Miller—or as we lovingly refer to him, Grandpa Bob—had been one of the most influential people in my life and had shown me what it meant to follow Jesus. I knew that if I called him, he'd pray and he'd get others praying as well. Even though it was the middle of the night, I knew he'd be on his knees in prayer for the souls of every person I came in contact with. This was no longer a tragedy, but a mission to lead others to the saving grace of Jesus Christ. When I called, my grandma, Jane, answered. She assured me that they would be praying.

As some nurse's aides came in and began rolling equipment out of my hospital room and the nursing staff started getting me set up with a catheter so I could do some hard-core bed rest, my hero walked in. Seeing Calvin was such a boost. He had gotten his sister, Stacey, to come and watch Ariana for the remaining hours of the night and had called in to let his boss know that he would need someone to cover for him so he could be with me in the hospital.

After explaining to him the details of my circumstances and what the plan of action was, he was just overwhelmed with joy that our baby was still alive. There were still several factors and details that needed to play out, but at that point in time, our baby's heart was beating—probably not for long, but Jesus was at work in that hospital room. Now, all we had to do was wait; easy, right? Or so I thought.

> "And we know that in all things God works for the good of those
> who love him, who have been called according to his purpose."
>
> &❧ ROMANS 8:28

....

Calvin stayed with me the entire night. I was so glad that he was there because I started experiencing something I hadn't anticipated: physical pain. I had been determined to lie completely still so as to allow for maximum healing of the amniotic sac. It was pure resolve that kept me absolutely still for fear that the smallest movement would cause a further tear. Even as I felt the fluid continue to trickle, I didn't flinch. With this stationary and somewhat upside down position (my head slanted toward the floor and feet elevated), I started to experience excruciating pain in my back. I think of myself as a pretty tough cookie; when my first daughter was born, I delivered her without the aid of any kind of pain reliever. Nope, not even Tylenol. And because my pain tolerance was quite established, this pain in my back took me for a loop. Medication was not a comfortable thing for me because I'd had a few experiences of being over-medicated, and it had left me feeling jittery and out of control, so to be considering asking for some at that point was quite odd.

I kept thinking, "I can make it. I can do it . . . if only I could switch the pressure from one cheek to the other . . . what if my baby loses more fluid because I move? I can endure this if it might save her . . . but can I keep lying still? Just one more minute, no, I can do it, I can do it . . . I can't do it, God, help me!" The pain surged on. I felt like such a sissy. Was I really going to ask for medication for pain that was brought on by lying absolutely still? I hadn't even received any medication during childbirth; surely that pain had been worse . . . but I wasn't so sure. Trying to redirect my thoughts didn't work either; the pain was just too intense. As it grew worse, my eyes filled with water and Calvin urged me to consider taking some medicine. Finally, I relented.

When the first medication didn't even scrape the tip of my pain, I was given a narcotic, but when my speech and vision slurred and my pain persisted, I decided that no medication was the better option.

Calvin stayed loyally by my side and comforted me throughout the night. Early the next morning, he had to relieve his sister who had been caring for Ariana, which left me alone with my pain and with my thoughts. I'm not sure which was worse, the pain or the thoughts. The glaringly low percentage of success with this procedure loomed heavily over me, especially with the intense pain I was experiencing. "Will I go through all of this pain only to have my baby die in the end?" Sorrow swept over me. Before, I had come to terms with the fact that my baby was going to die, but now, now there was this sliver of hope that she'd make it. To lose her all over again . . . how dreadful. I decided not to dwell on that and to shift my thinking in a different direction.

One of the nurses had told me that if my baby did die and I ended up delivering her at this point in my pregnancy, I would be able to hold her miniature body for as long as I wanted before saying goodbye to her. The thought was comforting, as I hadn't had a chance to see my previous baby that had miscarried. "Who was that little person?" I'd often wondered, "What did he or she look like? What color were the baby's hair and eyes?" But I had always found comfort in the knowledge that God had used my miscarriage to glorify Himself through our Christlike reaction, and that our little one was safe in His arms. That is what I decided to focus on while I lay in bed this time.

Then, a startling question entered my mind. "Do you have a funeral for preterm babies? Do they throw the body away or do we bury it? If we bury it, she'll need a headstone and name . . . " With this line of questions came a new sense of determination to find the perfect name for our precious girl. How was she to be remembered? Since I was only four months pregnant, we hadn't decided on any names, or even begun our list to choose from. We had only just begun acknowledging that I was pregnant.

One name I remember considering was Julene. My doctor's name was Julene, and what a lady she was! It was amazing that she had not left me to wait in the ER the night before only to end up with no fluid and a dead baby, as some doctors might have done. Instead, she had treated me as though this little baby was precious and deserved every chance at life, even though the likelihood of success was dismal. Yes, she was worthy to be named after. "Baby Jules, that has a nice ring to it," I thought, "But there is that small possibility she will live . . . do I want that to be her name even if she makes it? Do I name her one name if she dies because of the significance, but choose another if she makes it?" I felt guilty for even thinking those thoughts. How could I choose a name based on whether she lived or died? The names continued to swirl around in my mind along with other thoughts like, "If you do have funerals for these premature babies, what does a baby funeral look like? Do you invite people? Is it just family? Do they prepare the body? Are there caskets that small? How are we going to pay for it?"

As the questions spun in my mind, I handed them over one by one to my God. Once again, peace was bestowed upon my hurting body. I had pain, there were innumerous unknowns, but in the midst was a tranquility that I cannot explain. If my baby made it, my joy and amazement could not be matched, but if she died, I had every confidence that she'd be in the protective arms of my Savior, that He'd use her situation to reveal Himself to others, and that in the end I'd be reunited with her for eternity in Heaven! I longed to know exactly how God was going to use me. Would I ever know? Maybe a nurse would be touched and then seek Jesus through avenues I would never know about, or maybe someone would ask me to lead them to Christ right in my hospital room. I knew that I might never know the impact that this situation would make on others, but the important thing was to allow Christ to carry me and know that I was doing the right thing. With all things considered, this was a win-win situation.

When one of the nurses came to check on me, I asked her some of the questions that had been occupying my mind that morning, and she was so sweet to answer them all in turn. "Yes, you bury your baby if it is born prematurely." "You can have a ceremony for her, it just depends on what you choose. They do have little caskets and headstones for these little ones as well." My heart felt just a bit lighter with her answers. Even though I knew it would be a stretch for us to afford a funeral for our little girl, the thought of her being "disposed of" was unbearable.

3

Daybreak

WHEN CALVIN ARRIVED LATER IN the day to check on me, my mouth began to spill all that my head had been processing while he was away. His response to my thoughts was less than comforting. "Why do we have to have a casket? I'm not having a funeral for someone I don't even know. Why do we have to have a name? It's an unborn baby. They can just take care of it." His remarks were so cold and hurtful. How could he really think those thoughts? Or was I the one being too sentimental? Was I crazy? She *had* to have a name! Didn't she? The thought of her being nameless was unimaginable to me. The silence in the room was deafening. The stabbing pain of Calvin's remarks brought tears to my eyes. No amount of self-control or resolve was going to keep the flood of emotions I was feeling in check. I cried in silence as Calvin sat there in what I thought to be cold-hearted stillness.

What I didn't know then and can't bear to not tell you now is that Calvin was dealing with his own unbearable sense of loss of his precious unborn baby girl. He was unable to articulate the words and process his emotions after I had just spilled an immeasurable amount of information on his already heavy heart. He had been caring for our one-and-a-half-year-old daughter that day, worrying about me and my health, our unborn baby and her status, trying to figure out how he was going to pay the hospital bills I would rack up in only two days while on bed rest in the hospital, and he was just physically and emotionally exhausted. Coping with making funeral arrangements was the last thing on his agenda, and making the plans meant that he'd have to face the fact that his baby was going to die. Calvin is an incredibly loving and caring man, but this new, overwhelming amount of information was more than he could handle or process in that moment, and so he clammed up.

The rest of my time on bed rest at the hospital was very difficult for me. I went through spurts of completely handing my situation over to God and experiencing the rest and peace that only comes through Him, and then other spurts of letting worry, guilt, physical pain, and ache I felt from Calvin's words, steal my peace. These phases repeated over and over again in a constant battle. In order to retain my sanity, I had to hand my situation over to Christ second by second. The only reason I continued to do it was because I was only "OK" when God occupied my mind and heart.

Calvin continued to come and tried to offer support throughout the last day and a half that I was in the hospital, but the fact that he was unwilling to help me come up with a name for our baby was so disturbing to me. I knew that we were running out of time; soon, our little one would be here and we'd need a name to put on a headstone. I knew she would die because I could feel the liquid continue to flow out of my body, which meant that the sac had not healed.

I believed strongly that husbands were the head of the house and I tried very hard to respect Calvin and all of his decisions, but this one issue of naming our baby, I wrestled and prayed over the most while I was in the hospital. Would it tear us apart to decide whether or not to name her and to put the money out for her to be buried? I just kept handing it over to Christ and asking him to bring unity to mine and Calvin's thoughts. I also prayed that even with everything we were going through, Calvin and I would be used as a tool to bring others to the saving grace of Jesus Christ. It seemed impossible that we'd come to an agreement, but all I could do was give it all, every piece of it, to Jesus.

....

Sunday morning, the second full day of my hospitalization, dawned, and with it came the ultrasound that would check to see if my sac had healed.

I had already come to the conclusion that it hadn't, because I continued to feel fluid leaking. I knew that our baby was going to die, but was at perfect peace as God's grace continued to cover and protect me. As my doctor readied the machine, Calvin and I braced ourselves for the news that was only seconds away.

The doctor placed the monitor on my stomach and we waited in silence—first for a heartbeat, and second for a fluid measurement. I really had no idea what to expect. Two days had just been devoted to the cause of healing my womb, but because I could tell that it had not healed, I wasn't really sure what it could mean at this point. Would our baby still be alive? As adrenaline pumped through my body and caused me to shake, a rush of heat shot through me and brought sweat under my arms and legs and lower back, but at the same time I was freezing cold and shook with shivers so intense that my teeth chattered. What was happening to me? "God!" with eyes squeezed shut, screaming out in my mind, I called on the Creator of the universe once again. "Help me! I don't know if I can handle this!" I felt like my insides were going through the spin cycle of a washing machine and didn't know how to stop it or catch the side to hang on! I took a deep breath and waited for what the ultrasound would reveal about our unborn child.

The heartbeat came! What a wonderful and unexpected sound! I had lain so still and done my absolute best to do everything in my power to aid the healing of my womb. I had even learned to eat and drink while fighting gravity with my head slanted downward, and even though I had remained motionless, I had worried that my baby would die. Now, I knew she was alive! What a relief. But the thrill of the good news didn't have a chance to soak in before we received some not-so-good news: "There's only 0.6 centimeters of fluid left," my doctor said. My mind repeated what had just been announced, "*zero* point six." There was basically nothing left, only drops. But just as quickly as the terrible news came, God's grace and peace was there to pick me up. Pure calm and understanding washed over me, and I instantly felt ready to face whatever lay ahead. With the official news that my sac had not healed and the fluid was gone came details. My doctor began debriefing me for what to expect.

"Jen, your baby is going to die." I could tell that Dr.Hicks' announcement was hard for her to make. Her brown eyes were watering and she was staring at me with a deep sense of empathy. Before she could go on, I grabbed her hand and with tears in my own eyes, I whispered, "It's OK. We're going to be OK. God has this all in His hands." When Dr. Hicks blinked, more tears flipped off of her lashes, and as she wiped the remaining drops away, she took a deep breath and began explaining again the list of symptoms I was about to experience. "We are going to send you home now, and in a matter of days, you'll start to experience miscarriage-like symptoms. When that happens, come in and we'll deliver your baby. Just in case, in the meantime," Dr. Hicks continued, "I'd like to refer you to a specialist called an MFM (Maternal Fetal Medicine) doctor to analyze your pregnancy to see if they have any helpful tips for you." Then, kneeling next to my bed, she looked into my eyes and with a squeeze of my hand and a warm smile, she warned me, "Jen, this is a Catholic hospital, so we will not offer abortion to you here, but I want you to know, as soon as you visit a specialist, they will suggest that you terminate your pregnancy." I appreciated her honesty and forewarning against such possibilities. Her moral code and her eagerness to encourage were the reasons I had chosen her to be my doctor.

After Dr. Hicks had finished giving me the list of things to expect, I had a question of my own. I just had to know what our chances were in a medical sense. "So, there's no possibility that my baby can make it without fluid?" I asked.

"No," Dr. Hicks sighed. She looked into my eyes and continued, "Without fluid, the organs will all shut down one at a time. If you were further in your pregnancy or had some amount of fluid left, I'd say there might be a shot, but you're only 18 weeks along and the lungs don't even *start* to develop until 18 weeks. At 18 weeks gestation the lungs have not even begun to function. They require fluid to flow through them to inflate, much like oxygen, in order to develop them. The same is true of the kidneys. The baby needs to swallow the amniotic fluid, which will then pass through the kidneys and bladder, which in turn creates more amniotic fluid in order to repeat the cycle until all the organs are functioning. Without the fluid, your baby doesn't have a chance."

As Dr. Hicks finished her sentence a nurse walked in to take out my catheter, but before she could begin working, Dr. Hicks surprised me with a question: "Jen, would you mind praying? I just love to hear you pray!" I was caught off guard, but of course I wanted to pray—and how amazing that God had allowed for this nurse to join us! So with Calvin, Dr. Hicks, and Nurse Pepper gathered around my hospital bed, we joined hands, and bowed our heads as I proclaimed a prayer of thanks for all God was doing in our lives and in the lives of each person in the room. As I lifted my head and opened my eyes, I noticed that both Dr. Hicks and Nurse Pepper's eyes were filled with tears, and Calvin's eyes were filled with love; an adoring smile brightened his face and eyes as he looked down at me. Then Dr. Hicks turned to Nurse Pepper and said, "See! I told you she was good!"

I wasn't quite sure what to do with a compliment like "You pray good," because I was just talking with Jesus and don't really feel that's something that can be rated. But I smiled and thanked her; I was very grateful for an opportunity for my love for Jesus to flow out and hopefully touch the lives of those in the room.

A short while later, after my catheter had been removed, I was given a pamphlet on miscarriages and reminded to call Dr. Hicks' office if I started going into labor. Then Calvin and I were left alone in my hospital room to finish packing up my stuff and head home. It was at that point that I got the phone call that would change my perspective on everything.

It was my dad on the phone. "Jen! You're not going to believe what happened this weekend!" he announced excitedly, and then continued, " I had been praying for you the night that you called to tell me that you were in the hospital, then, the next morning, the teens and sponsors were meeting for morning worship and I felt led to share your prayer request. I said simply that you were in the hospital because your water had broken, that your baby was most likely going to die, but that you'd like for us to pray that God would use you and your situation to lead others to Him. I added that you were at peace because you know that your baby is headed to Heaven to lie in the arms of Jesus, and I asked the group how many of them were ready for Heaven. Then, I asked the kids if they knew where they'd be going when they died," he paused for just a moment to catch his breath.

"Jen, I could not have expected what happened next. We prayed for you and it turned into a time of prayer at the altar. The teens poured to the front and laid their petitions there. When the prayer time came to an end, teens started randomly sharing their testimonies and different things that they were experiencing in their lives at that point. One young girl named Molly came up to the mic and began sharing her story. She said that she had never been to a church event before, but came this weekend only because her friend invited her. When she brought up what I had said about you, Jen, she started to cry. She shared about how she had been left by her father when she was 10 years old and had undergone abuse and neglect and could not understand the peace that you have with your situation.

"She went on to say that she realized that God was the father that would never leave her, that would provide peace and protection. She couldn't imagine how all you were thinking about is other people's salvation while your little baby is basically on her deathbed. Molly said that she wanted that kind of love and peace from God and that she had made a choice to accept Jesus as her Lord and Savior that morning!" my dad exclaimed with excitement. "God is moving here, Jen. Molly's words brought others forward who then shared their stories, and these kids' lives were touched. Our service went two hours over! It was amazing. You didn't know it when you asked me for prayer, Jen, that your situation would bring revival up here!"

I didn't know what to say. God had answered my prayer that people would see Him in my situation! I thought I might never even know if anything I had done would impact others for the Lord, and here, only two days into it, one young woman had accepted Jesus as her Lord and Savior! At that moment, in my mind, God's purpose for this situation was fulfilled, for my little baby was going to be in Heaven—and because of her little life, so was Molly! The emotion that flooded my heart was overwhelming. God was using this situation in a much larger way than I had ever anticipated! I had thought it would be absolutely worth it if only one person came to eternal salvation through our situation, and here, an entire revival was sparked in our youth group in the mountains! I looked over at Calvin and just had to share with him what had just happened in McCall.

After retelling Calvin what my dad had told me, he looked at me with watery eyes and said, "Wow, Jen. This is our precious little baby, and she is touching countless lives." It was apparent that God had let Calvin in on the peace that I had been feeling. The big picture was being unveiled before his eyes even as we faced the loss of our precious little child whom we hadn't even welcomed into the world yet. The news of lives being changed in our youth group couldn't have come at a better time. We were being discharged from the hospital with a spiritual boost, and both Cal and I were on the same page! God's blessings come in all forms, but this one, I knew, was a miracle.

4

Jesus Take the Wheel

IT FELT WONDERFUL TO BE home and hug on my sweet little Ari. I had missed her so much. The hard part though, was wondering just how involved to be. I was carrying a little baby that was, at the moment, alive, but was doomed to die within a few days. It seemed odd to be up and around doing my normal activities and just waiting for my body to go into labor, especially when I had just come from an atmosphere of complete resolve to get this child here safely no matter the cost. I desperately wanted to dance and play with my little Ariana, but everything about being "up" felt wrong. For one thing, my body was in total disarray. I was completely disoriented from being tilted upside down for two days and also felt very weak. Whenever I stood up it felt like I was going to fall, so I crashed on the couch for the first few moments after being home. I couldn't believe how exhausted I felt.

Those few moments turned into hours. My body was utterly wiped out from the pain and stress it had just experienced at the hospital. Calvin took care of our little girl as I rested and tried to gain strength and balance enough to function. One thing that caused me frustration was that I couldn't walk normally or stand for moments without help. My body had totally placed itself back on bed rest. As I lay on the couch that day, I realized that during my stay in the hospital, I had been pumped with IV fluids to try and keep my body hydrated as well as replenish fluid to the amniotic sac. With that realization, I felt an urgency to hydrate, so I filled my ginormous (that's a Jennifer word for huge) mug full of water. It seems that all I did that day and the next was lie on the couch and sip water. Whenever I'd run out, Cal would get more.

After two days at home, it was time to visit the MFM specialist. I had no idea what to expect. Supposedly, our child had died and needed to be delivered. Because Calvin didn't have anymore time off from work, my mom took me to the doctor, while my mother-in-law kept Ariana. In the case that our baby *was* ready to be delivered today, Calvin would take a personal day and join me. The ride to the doctor's office was somewhat somber. I had completely given my situation to Jesus, but it did not take away the emotion of going through the loss of my sweet little babe. Every human bone in my body cried out at the loss of her. With all my heart, I wanted to keep our precious little one, but I did not want anything that was not within the will of God.

As my emotions ran wild, a song came on the radio that calmed me right down to my core. It's a song by Carrie Underwood called "Jesus, Take the Wheel." The words of the song tell a story about a young woman traveling by car in the snow to visit her parents on Christmas Eve. With her little baby in the backseat, she drove with her mind on her rough year, and without noticing, she was driving way too fast. Before she knew it, she was spinning on black ice. The song describes her emotions like this: "She saw both their lives flash before her eyes, she didn't even have time to cry, she was so scared, and she threw her hands up in the air" The words described how I was feeling on the way to the doctor that day. I had no control of what was going to happen to me or my baby, but the lines that came next are what took my breath away: "Jesus, take the wheel!" The words floated out of the speakers and into my heart. "Jesus take the wheel!" my heart uttered as peace melted over my body.

I took a deep breath, and then exhaled, "Jesus, take the wheel. Don't let me drive, God. I cannot do this on my own. I need you," I whispered. The song finished as we pulled into the parking space at the specialist's office. After inhaling deeply, my mom and I got out of the car and took the walk into the building, but I had found a new sense of peace and felt ready for what I was about to go through.

Once inside, checked in, and sitting next to yet another ultrasound machine, we were ready to find out what had happened with my baby.

Many women would have loved to get as many ultrasounds as I was getting of my unborn baby, but considering the circumstances, the ultrasounds were unnerving and caused my heart to beat wildly within my chest. Once everything was set up and ready, we waited for a few moments before getting to meet my MFM doctor. Mom was so awesome; she had given up her free day to come with me and offer support when I needed it the most. I don't remember if many words were exchanged during our time of waiting in that room, but I do remember the feeling of complete love and sympathy she offered. After a short wait, Dr. Striker came in. He was very cold and impersonal in comparison with my OB-GYN, but I thought, "This is only one time, and then I'll be done with him and can go back to *my* doctor."

Dr. Striker squirted the warm goo onto my stomach and spread it out with the ultrasound probe. Here we were, waiting yet again for answers via ultrasound. This time, however, we were checking to see how my body was handling the miscarriage. I was not as nervous as at my last ultrasound in the hospital, when we were checking to see if our baby had died. I already knew what to expect this time, and there was no remaining hope that our little one was alive. All that remained was peace about what had happened and the readiness to carry out delivering our dead baby. It sounds very strange that I felt peace about such a terrible thing, but I really did. God's love completely coated my heart, and I felt ready to handle anything.

To our great surprise, and my doctor's, we heard a heartbeat I don't know how to fully express how much we were caught off guard, but it was like an atomic bomb had just gone off, and the whole room went silent as the ripple from the explosion slowly traveled the distance of the room until the *boom* reached us, and we all jumped! Shock took hold of me. "How could this be?" I wondered. I had been sure that our baby would die, because, according to my thinking, our baby was going to die in order to bring glory to God. Wouldn't her death coupled with (hopefully) our supernatural peace bring God more glory than her simply being born? Well, I wasn't going to complain. This was a miracle. I was not sure why God had chosen to let her little heart beat that day, but selfishly, I was glad.

Another blow came directly after finding out that she was still alive. My doctor turned to me and said, "Your situation is not good." Well, *that*

I knew. Of course my situation was not *good*. A baby living in no fluid, with no chance to develop the rest of her vital organs, was not a "good situation." "Tell me something I *don't* know," I thought.

He continued by saying, "Well, with no fluid, there's not really a chance for her to survive. You are playing a game of Russian roulette right now. With your womb open and susceptible to outside bacteria, your chances of contracting an infection are very high. In fact, it's only a matter of time until infection sets in. You are very lucky that infection has not come in the past two days; many women become infected within the first few hours of having their water broken. Normally, we induce labor in full-term pregnancies after the water breaks because we don't want the womb open and exposed for over 24 hours." His cold blue eyes pierced mine and I could tell that there was no life in them. After a moment's pause, he continued, "My medical recommendation is that we go ahead and terminate this pregnancy," he said matter-of-factly.

What had he just said? He had already continued to his next sentence, but my mind was stuck on the previous one . . . was he making plans to "terminate my pregnancy"? Was this a choice or an order? I needed to *terminate* my pregnancy? *Terminate*? As in, *abort*? No. No! This was *not* an option. As a young adolescent, after learning all about abortion from a wonderful Sunday school teacher, I was vehemently against it. I had vowed at my young age that no matter the circumstance, even if it were a case of rape or if my life were on the line, I would not abort. Ever. It is one thing for a doctor to clean out your womb if the baby has already died, but it is entirely another to kill a living being and then clean it out. I did not believe that God gave us the power to take another life into our own hands, and I was n``ot about to do that with my own young child.

"No," I said rather firmly. "No?" He looked at me with questioning eyes. "No, I will not terminate this pregnancy," I stated concretely. His eyes narrowed as he looked at me, trying to figure out where in the world I was coming from. It was as if he was thinking, "Who in their right mind would put their life at stake for a tiny fetus that isn't even alive yet?" And then, a new look spread across his face. All of a sudden he was looking at me as if I were a young child whom he was about to make understand his argument in simpler terms: "Your body will never take this pregnancy to term; in fact, it's only a matter of time before it rejects the child within you. There is no chance that this baby will ever live, and in the meantime, you are exposing yourself to harmful bacteria that could kill you. Do you understand? *You* could die. The infection that could attack in this area of your body is *that* harmful," he spoke like he had just nailed his case and signed off on the verdict. But his attempt to put it into simpler terms had not worked, and I again surprised him with the word "No," and continued, "I absolutely in no circumstance will abort this baby," I said resolutely.

Now, with frustration, Dr. Striker's eyebrows creased and eyes narrowed, as he spoke down to me, "I don't think you understand; this is doctor's orders and your life is at stake." He continued with no beating around the bush, "There is absolutely no chance that your baby will make it. It would be foolish to risk your life to save this one." "Well," I responded with more grace and peace than I thought I could ever possess as I smiled up at him, "This life is not mine to take. I believe in a huge God that can work miracles and if He wills it, this baby will live. If not, she will die and be with Him. But either way," I paused and drew air into my lungs as I held back tears, "Either way," I continued, "my baby's life is in His hands as well as my life." That was the most freeing sentence I had ever spoken because now . . . now, this was not just about glorifying God, but truly giving it *all* to Him—even to the extent of my life! Dr. Striker gave me a look of pure disgust and pity, and then said, "If you do get an infection, you won't have a choice; we *will* take the baby to save your life." There was only silence for a moment, and then I retorted, "Then I'll pray that that doesn't happen because I'll never consent to an abortion." He just stared at me, absolutely puzzled.

For a moment, Dr. Striker left the room and I was sent to the restroom to give a urine sample. While I was gone, the nurse that had been standing in the back of the room, apparently moved by the entire exchange between the doctor and me, approached my mom and breathed one simple sentence to her, "Wow, she's quite an old 23-year-old, isn't she." My mom replied, "Yes, she is," and they waited quietly as the seriousness of the news was still trying to make its way through both of their minds.

After analyzing my urine, they found that, miraculously, infection had not set in during the two days I had been at home. Since I had decided not

"What?" I asked again, longing to know what was rolling around in his mind.

"You could die! What if you died? Then, it would just be me and . . . and Ari. What am I supposed to do?" he burst out and then turned away from me in a moment of heated emotion and anger.

For the first time, I felt guilty for choosing life for my unborn child. And then I felt guilty for even considering *not* choosing life, because that meant abortion . . . and I couldn't, just couldn't even say the word aloud. It went against the very fibers of my being, against who I had professed to be, to myself and the world . . . no, I couldn't abort her. My blood started to pump and the thoughts raced on.

"Am I wrong? Would God want me to abort her to be unselfish and to care for my little girl and husband?" Thoughts continued spinning, "No, how can I even think that . . . *no!*" Gasping, I tried to continue processing, "What is Calvin thinking? Is he terrified for my life and for what his will be like without me? I guess I didn't take the doctor's words seriously . . . will it really get to the point of having to choose my life or hers?" As my thoughts started to spin out of control, my mouth opened without asking my mind for consent, and I blurted out, "Calvin, how could you say that? Do you want me to abort our baby?" I breathed in deeply then, with tears spilling over the brims of my eyes.

He stood there for a moment, cold and still. And then in a flood of compassion, he looked at me and said in a low, calm voice, "No, Jen. I'm just afraid. I don't want to lose you, but we can't abort our baby. You did the right thing," and then he lowered his eyes again and took the pose which I knew to be his position of prayer.

My blood pressure lowered some as I looked at this big, strong man who was my husband. He sat at our kitchen table hunched over with his head bowed and forehead resting on intertwined fingers in prayer. If a heart could literally break and feel the pain of the pieces shattering, that's what mine was doing at that moment. I knew he loved me, our daughter Ariana, and our unborn baby more than he knew how to express, and all he wanted to do was to take care of us, but in that instant he knew that he was completely and totally out of control. He was dealing with this whole situation in his own way and I knew that I needed to give him space to process and seek help from his Savior.

....

Having decided that abortion was not an option and that I would do what I could to give this baby a chance as long as she was alive, I put myself on bed rest. I know, pretty crazy and unheard of; but I felt strongly that God wanted me horizontal because with every moment that I stood upright, fluid was leaking from my womb and decreasing her chances. After all, God had made me a promise that my baby was going to make it. I hadn't shared that secret promise with anyone for fear they'd think I was insane or naïve, because the doctors had clearly told me that she was as good as dead. So, I kept my secret promise to myself and tried to do my part in giving our precious baby her best shot at life.

The decision to stay "down" caused quite a bit of work for Calvin and our extended family. Because Calvin had to continue to work his job *and* manage all of the household chores that I had done in the past, everyone chipped in to help. Our Sunday school class at church started coming with meals that fed us for the entire week, while my mom, mother-in-law, aunt, cousins, and friends all took turns helping me with Ari while Calvin was at work. It was absolutely humbling to watch as people flooded in to help us through this time of waiting.

Even with people helping, though, Calvin had considerably more on his plate now than ever before. At first, Calvin had seemed OK with the extra load, but as responsibilities stacked on top of obligations and housework, it began to eat away at him. Every day Calvin woke up at midnight to do his devotions, eat breakfast, and get off to work. After work, he'd come straight home around two o'clock in the afternoon to relieve whoever was helping me with Ariana that day. He'd do the dishes that had accrued, followed by laundry, playing with Ari, serving Ari and me our dinners, getting Ari ready for bed and tucking her in, and then crashing later than normal at seven o'clock, only to start the day all over again at midnight.

To top it all off, Calvin had a very physically demanding job. He worked as a delivery driver for a company that delivered food to restaurants. Every day, Calvin drove a huge semi truck that was packed to the gills with food and manually unloaded the food and wheeled it into the restaurants. Thousands of pounds of food passed through my husband's hands each day. To return to a home that required more work and the emotional involvement it takes to care for a one-year-old must've been tremendously difficult, but he did it. Day in and day out, Calvin managed to perform every task placed before him.

Guilt was my constant companion as I watched Calvin and others doing my normal duties. Some people might consider this time a nice break for me, but it was quite the opposite. Anyone who has been bedridden or helpless will identify that it is almost a demeaning feeling to have others do for you, or do the things that you should be doing. Humiliation is another word I would use to describe this time when I had to *admit* that I needed help! I desperately wanted to play with my little Ari and attain the self worth that comes from keeping a home clean and comfortable. Every time Calvin would refill my water, serve me a meal, or do one of my chores, my whole gut would churn because I knew he was exhausted and there was really nothing physically keeping me down on that couch. I wasn't going to die if I stood up. I wasn't sick and didn't feel ill, weak, or nauseous. It was so unnatural for me to just lie there with no visible reason. But I knew in my heart that it was absolutely necessary for our tiny baby that lay within my unstable body.

And I think Calvin felt sometimes like I was perfectly capable of doing everything on my own, but was choosing to lie still and wait for the inevitable to happen—for our baby to die. Calvin definitely hadn't been given the knowledge that our baby was going to make it, because with each passing day that he had two full-time jobs (his own, accompanied by all of mine), it seemed his anger and bitterness towards me grew worse.

"Why doesn't she just get up and help me?" Cal later confessed that he had thought. "The baby is just going to die and then all of this time will have been wasted." As his anger burned, my guilt heightened. Some days, I'd try to get up and do things for Ariana to help him out, but then huge gushes of fluid would escape and leave my baby with little to no water, which would also wrack me with guilt. For me, it was a lose-lose situation. If I helped Calvin, I lost because I'd lose fluid, bringing my baby closer to death; but if I stayed down on the couch to help my baby have as much fluid as possible, I lost with Calvin because he was left with the workload and was angry with me.

Having people come to help with Ari was hard, too. It was a lifesaver and absolutely necessary, but it was difficult to take my hands off of my mommy responsibilities. Before my water broke, Ariana and I spent all day every day together baking treats for Daddy, playing with her toys, or singing and dancing to the local Christian music station. Her latest favorite had been dancing to the VeggieTales singing the Hokey Pokey. Before my water broke, she'd run to me with lit up eyes and overflowing energy and say, "Hoka hoka hoka pokie!" which meant that she wanted to listen to the song and dance around to it. So, we'd listen to those crazy VeggieTales sing their version of the song while we danced around throwing our arms and legs and lips and tongues *in* until we'd had enough! But now, being unable to do that with a ruptured sac brought more guilt and frustration than I know how to express.

....

Being on bed rest had proven to be difficult, but there was one way that I had found to pass the time. While Calvin was at work and Ari was playing with whoever came for the day, I read my Bible. In that time of desperation, the Bible came to life like never before and truly became a source of nourishment to my soul. God reminded me whenever I was in His word of the ways that He was still blessing me. After all, every single day since I had been on bed rest, He had brought the perfect person to come and care for Ariana, and meals had come like clockwork so that neither Calvin nor I had to cook!

Worries always tried to attack. When Ariana would come to snuggle with me, she'd sometimes jump up on the couch and crawl on me, which was not good for the baby because she had no fluid to protect against outside bumps and thumps, so I would worry that Ari was hurting her. Ari had also become angry with me for not getting up and playing with her, enough that she would hit me. It broke my heart to see her so distressed with her situation.

But God was so good about soothing each of my fears and worries. He brought dear friends and family in to help Ari stay occupied and get her mind off of me, and I ended up with hours of just lying on the sofa, reading the Bible. It was an excellent way to pass my time and to maintain optimism in the midst of devastation.

On many occasions I would read something eye-opening or really significant and save it all day to share with Calvin, only for him to shoot it down when he got home. It was a constant battle for me to keep optimistic, fight away feelings of guilt, stay motivated to stay down, and not fold under each attack from the evil one, but through it all, I felt the hand of God guiding me. I knew that the path I had chosen was the one God wanted me on. God urged me to take my concerns about Calvin to Jesus and to release my fears and frustrations so that He could take care of the rest.

....

Each day that passed was like an eternity. I remember one day in particular when I had not felt my baby move at all, which had become my alarm that something might be wrong. Feeling my baby move was the only way I knew that she was still alive, so when Calvin got home, we all got into our little white Honda Civic and drove to my doctor's office to see if our baby was still living. It was the second-longest drive I had ever experienced, next to my first drive to the hospital when my water broke. At this point, I had been on bed rest for one week, and it was very likely that our baby's time had run out.

As Dr. Hicks prepared to place the Doppler onto my stomach, which was smaller than normal because of the lack of fluid, Calvin and I both held our breath. This was it. We were about to find out if our little one's time here was finished. I had no idea what to think. I had felt so sure that she was going to make it, but not once that day had I felt her move. It was too good to be true to think that a baby could make it after having the water break at only four months of pregnancy. Before my water broke, my stomach had barely begun to "show." By all accounts, this would be considered a miscarriage because of the early gestational age of the baby. How could I have thought that she could ever make it? "Impossible," my head told me as the doctor made ready to put the ultrasound probe on my little tummy.

As the doctor lowered the probe to rest on my abdomen, my heart beat so loudly I thought she might hear it. Calvin grabbed my hand in a gesture of love and support; it was small signals like this that indicated to me that his love was still there, even though his attitude and words were sometimes harsh. He gave my hand another squeeze as we both took a deep breath and waited to find out if our baby had finally gone to meet Jesus.

"Finally, be strong in the Lord and in his mighty power. Put on the full armor of God so that you can take your stand against the devil's schemes. For our struggle is not against flesh and blood, but against the rulers, against the authorities, against the powers of this dark world and against the spiritual forces of evil in the heavenly realms."

ॐ Ephesians 6:10-12

6

Preparing My Field

It had been a relief to hear my baby's little heart beat once again, but I fought with all my might to keep my mind and heart in a place of peace and devotion to God. Every second I was on bed rest was a challenge. The evil one filled my mind with fears, lies, and doubt that God would keep His promise to save my baby. With scares like the one a few weeks earlier when I hadn't felt my baby move for an entire day, the opportunity for doubt and fear presented itself quite often. The battle really was in each second. The seconds turned into minutes, minutes into hours, hours into days, and days into weeks.

Each week I visited Dr. Striker so that he could perform an ultrasound to check the baby's status, my fluid levels, and the baby's growth. The fluid usually ranged from 1.0 to 2.5 centimeters, but never above. Dr. Striker's opinion had not changed, but he had learned not to voice it because my opinion had not changed either and my mind was made up. I would not abort my child. All we could do, from his point of view, was watch to make sure I didn't get an infection and make sure that the baby was living and growing each week. Occasionally, he'd remind me that even though my baby was growing, her inner organs were not being formed; she would be born with the shell of her body on target in terms of size, but with no necessary vital organs, and she would die at birth. It never changed my mind, just made me wonder how God was going to keep His promise.

worn, sorted them, washed them, and folded them. We also prepared her bassinet and blankets and arranged them neatly next to my bed. Calvin hadn't said much when he saw what we were doing, only glanced and then walked away. I knew he wasn't happy, but also knew that it was something that I had to do.

Then, a phone call came from Calvin's Aunt Doris. I had always felt very close to her as we talked frequently through e-mail and bonded on a deep level. She had called to encourage me and let me know that she had been praying that our little baby would be kept safe in the hands of our great and mighty God during my pregnancy, and that God had given her a peace that our baby was going to live. When she mentioned her peace, my heart skipped a beat. Wow. God was talking to this woman that I loved so dearly and had placed His calm and peace in her heart about my baby in the same way that He had done for me. I shared with her that I had been feeling the same way for several weeks. The conversation left me encouraged, uplifted, and ready to share with Calvin the promise that God had given to me.

Later that night, I told Calvin about the complete peace and knowledge that God had given me. I admitted that I believed our little baby was going to live and that his aunt had been experiencing the same peace about our situation. His response was somewhat surprising. "Jen, I have started to feel the same way. It's so unlikely, but I have really been feeling a peace lately that God is going to save her."

"You have?" I asked, surprised. "Yeah, I mean, I know it's not real probable, but that's how I've been feeling. You know," he continued, "I've felt at times like, if she's going to die, I wish she'd just do it so that we don't have to hurt anymore and it can all go away, but I don't *want* her to die and I feel so bad that those thoughts even came at all. I want her, Jen. I want her so badly," he breathed intensely. "Each day gets harder," he started. "With each day, we grow closer to getting her, and if we lose her now . . . " his voice trailed off. "I just don't know," was all he said.

His words had caught me off guard; his honesty was penetrating. I felt the same way. It was not a feeling of wanting to lose our baby, but with each passing day, we were losing time together, time as a family, time with Ariana. And if it was all going to end in our baby's death . . . If she was going to die, it would be easier not to get so attached, because with each second and each little movement this little baby made, Calvin and I both grew more and more madly in love with her. To lose her now would be . . . too much.

Calvin's admission to having peace about our baby's survival was overwhelming! Was God really going to give our baby life outside the womb? As improbable as it was, I really believed that He would.

....

My 24th week of gestation brought many unexpected pieces of news. The first was that our baby was still alive; that was the best "surprise" of all! But the second piece of information was that my pregnancy was becoming too risky, and that at any time I could become infected or go into labor, so Dr. Striker wanted me to check into the hospital to be monitored for the remainder of my pregnancy. When I brought that news home to Calvin, he was less than thrilled; in fact, a whole new set of worries came over him.

"How are we going to pay for you to stay in the hospital for the rest of your pregnancy? That could be 16 more weeks! And each day costs at least $1,000!" he assumed. "I know," I whispered, "I don't know how it will work or how we'll pay for it, but he said that I have to go to the hospital so that they can monitor me and the baby 24/7. I won't be in the hospital for 16 weeks though, they won't let me go that long. Dr. Striker said that no matter what, they will induce me at 34 weeks gestation because the risk at that point becomes too great, so at the most, we have 10 more weeks."

"How can they *make* someone go to the hospital and accrue bills? I don't get it," Calvin continued. "We'll have like a million dollars in bills even with our insurance." After pausing to do some real calculations, Calvin said, "We do have great insurance, but even with the insurance paying 90 percent, we'll still owe the 10 percent. And at $1,000 per day for 10 weeks, and figuring in the 10 percent, we'd still have to pay around $7,000 and that's not counting any procedures that may need to be done or the delivery of the baby, dead or alive. Where are we going to get that kind of money?" he asked, not really wanting an answer. Then he went on, "Jen, maybe we can just monitor you at home." I could tell he was thinking out loud. I knew my husband well enough to know that he'd need to process this new information for a few days, so I left him to think as I went to pray.

I knew in my heart that it was important for me to go to the hospital so that they could monitor the baby's heart rate and look for contractions to see the first sign of trouble for either me or the baby. All I could do now was to give the situation to my God and hope for the best. He had never let me down in the past, so I would continue to trust Him with all that I had, even with the life of our baby.

....

As I lay in the hospital bed, with a sore hind-end because of the recent injection of steroids I had received to help develop the lungs of my unborn baby, my mind raced at the way God had opened the doors for me to be there with my husband's consent. Calvin's heart had been completely softened and his eyes opened to the will of God. A few days after telling him that the doctors wanted me to go to the hospital, I had made a phone call to our insurance company to find out what kind of coverage we had. To my great surprise, I found out that our great insurance was really, *really* great. Not only were we only responsible for only 10 percent of the bills, but after we paid our deductible of $1,500, we would not be responsible for any other fees; our insurance would cover 100 percent after our deductible was met! With this amazing news, Calvin was on board and wanted me monitored at the hospital.

Watching God work in the past few weeks had been like watching a master artist at work, placing each detail on the paper in the perfect order. When Calvin started working for the food distribution service the year before, he had felt strongly that he needed to buy the premium insurance package. I had given him a hard time about selecting the more expensive package, but now as I was lying in the hospital racking up thousands of dollars of medical bills, I was so thankful that Calvin *had* trusted God's leading in purchasing the premium insurance plan. God had known all those months ago what was going to happen and provided just the right job with the exact right insurance that would save us from a life of medical debt! My husband was much more sensitive to the Holy Spirit than I ever gave him credit for. When he had selected the premium insurance, I had just seen our dollars floating out the window, but he was following the directing of Jesus as He was paving the way to financial freedom.

Even with the financial doors opening for me to be in the hospital, we had still had the question of what to do with Ariana while Calvin was working. And not only did Calvin work during the day, but in the middle of the night. What kind of daycare would be open from midnight to three or four o'clock in the afternoon? None. So, it was decided that Calvin and Ariana would stay with my parents while I was in the hospital so that Ariana could stay in bed and in the care of my parents when Calvin went to work in the middle of the night. And in the morning, my mom would take her to her new daycare on her way to teach her kindergarteners at the local Christian school. Our finances were rescued again when God provided the exact amount of money needed for Ariana's childcare in our 2008 tax returns that we had not yet spent!

....

Life continued at a rapid pace for Calvin: each morning at 12 a.m., Cal woke up and went to work. Then, at around 2:00 p.m., he got off of work, and since he worked in the neighboring city of Boise where I was in the hospital, he visited me each day. After visiting me, he went to our house and got the mail as well as took care of the yard and any other maintenance our house required, and then he picked up Ariana from daycare around 4:00 p.m. The minutes in Cal's day continued to spiral away as he made dinner for Ariana and himself, played with her, put her to bed, and got to bed himself around 8:00 p.m., leaving only four or five hours of sleep until he did it all over again.

7

Calvin

My mind reeled at the thought of how God had orchestrated every detail to bring us to this point, but it was all working out. For the past eight weeks, I had been on bed rest, seven of those at home. And every evening, we had a meal provided for us from a member of our Sunday school class! For seven weeks they brought food. For seven weeks, a friend or family member helped me with Ariana each and every day. For seven weeks, God sustained and cared for our unborn child. And in seven weeks, God promised me that He'd save our baby and gave Calvin a change of heart and the same amazing promise.

Now, when Calvin came to visit me each day, he was a new person, my best friend again. It had seemed ages since we could truly enjoy each other's company, but now, when he'd come to the hospital it was as if the time of trouble and anxiety had never happened. Now we were old souls enjoying peace and the love of Christ together. The worry and fear that our baby wouldn't make it still popped up frequently, but now we were both on the same page and armed against the devil's lies and evil attempts to cause discouragement and doubt.

> "Always be joyful. Pray continually and give thanks whatever happens. That is what God wants for you in Christ Jesus."
>
> 1 Thessalonians 5:16-18 (NCV)

At my admission to the hospital, I was given specific instructions that I would not receive some of the same privileges as other patients in the unit because I had no fluid in my womb. While others were allowed to stand and walk around or even to sit up, my orders were to lie flat and still. The doctors also required that any sick family stay away during my time in the hospital, because if I were to get sick, it could either mask an infection or give false signs of infection in my uterus. And if they saw any warning signs of an infection, the doctors would have to induce labor to take the baby, and my time on bed rest would end abruptly.

I was constantly aware of my surroundings and what I touched and didn't touch. If someone came to visit, but hadn't checked in at the front desk and innocently brought a cold or cough, I mentally took note of what they had touched so as to disinfect once they had left. Lying flat was nothing new, as I had already been horizontal for seven weeks prior at home. I was used to eating, drinking, reading, and doing any other activity on my back. All in all, I could abide by the restrictions that were given to me; it was the waiting that was unbearable, and the four walls that seemed to close in around me nearer and nearer with each passing day.

My time in the hospital was harder in some ways than my bed rest had been at home, and easier in other ways. Easier in the sense that it wasn't Calvin that was waiting on me; paid staff filled my water bottle, cleaned my bedding, and served my meals, so I didn't carry as much guilt as I had when I felt I was putting Calvin out. But it was oh, so much harder in the sense that I was 30 minutes away from Calvin and Ariana and all of my family!

My little Ari wasn't there to fill the room with lovely sounds of giggles and childish singing, or to snuggle up against me as we watched her favorite VeggieTales shows. I missed crawling into a warm bed with the love of my life and just being near my best friend, Calvin. Life was incredibly different in the hospital with bleach-scented sheets, nurses coming in around the clock to check my vital signs, and no sense of privacy whatsoever, but I knew that God was in it all. He had promised to be with me wherever I went, and so I rested in His love and provision each day and each second.

"Have I not commanded you? Be strong and courageous.
Do not be terrified; do not be discouraged, for the LORD
your God will be with you wherever you go."

❧ JOSHUA 1:9

....

To fill my time I read my Bible, worked on a Bible study that someone had brought to me, and read countless books. I also enjoyed working Sudoku puzzles that a family member had ingeniously thought to give me. There was a television set in my room, but I found it impossible to keep a positive mind and outlook when it was on. The world was too oppressive for the fragile emotional and spiritual state I was in. The evil one was constantly attacking me, trying to catch me off guard with a fatal blow to my faith, so my TV stayed off.

Each new day for me began with a shower, an early morning visit from my doctor, and breakfast. During the day I had three 30-minute sessions of monitoring of the baby and contractions with belts and sensors strapped around my abdomen. A cleaning woman came in daily to rid my room and bathroom of bacteria and germs, after which I'd have lunch, an afternoon visit from my doctor, and dinner. Nurses came in to take my vitals every three hours, day and night.

The abundant time I had on my hands to spend with Jesus just wasn't enough. I'd just get started on my Bible study when a staff member would come in to check on me, want to talk, or need to assess me. With entire days to just lie in bed, you'd think I'd have plenty of time to dive into Scripture, but with the many interruptions, I constantly craved more. God was sustaining my spirit and the life of my unborn child, but I just couldn't get enough of Jesus. His peace radiated through my life in such a way that I felt I was a human being living in a human struggle with supernatural power to overcome. The human emotions and weaknesses were ever present in me and sometimes arose like a wildfire, but Jesus' power and light in my life washed the doubt and fear away like fresh rain that extinguishes the fires of death and destruction.

I recently found a poem that I had written during my time on bed rest at the hospital and thought it appropriate to share here; it is titled "Bed Rest."

Stuck in a bed, Nothing to do, Head's in a blur, Can't tell what's true, Breakfast, lunch, dinner, Nurses here and there, Visitors in and out, No privacy anywhere, Eyes are burning, Back is stiff, Tasteless food, Life in a rift, Miss my family, Empty hours, Clock ticks on, I have no power, The Lord picks me up, Breathes new life, Restores my soul, Took away my strife, The joy floods in, He fills my heart, My cup runneth over, Ah, a new start

I was told later by one of the nurses that they all referred to my room as the "happy room." I had been placed in the antepartum wing of the hospital, which housed all the expectant mothers who had high-risk pregnancies. Most would probably deliver early and maybe never get to meet their children alive, so it wasn't exactly the happiest unit in the hospital. My room on the other hand, they said, was filled with hope and light.

There were times, though, that it all got to me. One night in particular, I'd been in the hospital for about a week and hadn't seen Ariana. With Cal's work schedule and everything else going on, my parents and Cal hadn't had a chance to drive Ariana the 30-minute distance for a visit. As I lay in my hospital bed in the dark, the tears came. I wept and wept as silently as I could so that the nurses wouldn't hear. I missed Ariana more than words could express. I had what I knew to be irrational fears that she would forget me or not love me anymore, or even worse, think that I didn't love her. I cried until the tears ran out and exhaustion took me to sleep. This was one of the few times that sorrow overtook my heart and caused me deep pain and loneliness, but most of the time, Calvin made special trips to visit me and bring me sweet gifts and company.

My favorite visit came one evening when Calvin was free to stay up because he wasn't scheduled to work the following day. He had planned a little hospital "date" for the two of us. Calvin surprised me with dinner, pizza that I had been craving, and some delicious apple pie and ice cream! What a great contrast the pizza was to the bland and ordinary food I received at the hospital!

Later, Calvin and I lay in my hospital bed together and watched a movie. I will never forget that night, as it was the most normal I'd felt in almost two months and the closest I'd gotten to be physically and emotionally with my dear husband. I loved it.

....

Coming up with a name for our precious baby had not been a major topic of conversation between Cal and me since he had put an abrupt end to it when I was in the hospital the first time. The fact that he had wanted to leave our baby nameless had been so difficult for me, but I thought that maybe he'd be more open to it now. I knew that Cal would be coming later in the day to spend some time with me. "Should I bring it up and see if he is open to it? Surely now, after all these weeks, we can't leave our baby nameless if she dies; and I can't name her all by myself!" I thought. Lately, my time had been spent pouring over books and baby-naming websites to find just the right one, but none really seemed to fit. My hope was that once Calvin and I worked together on naming her, the right one would come. It was at that moment that I committed the matter to prayer and lifted my concerns to our awesome Jesus who hears each petition and brings them to the throne of our Almighty God in intercession.

....

When Cal came to visit, usually he'd come in and sit on the chair next to my bed after dotting my lips with a sweet kiss, but today, he had a new spring in his step. He walked briskly over to me, leaned over my bed, and brushed my forehead with a light kiss. Then, to my great surprise, gentle words that I never thought I'd hear began flowing from his mouth.

"Jen, I love you," his eyes pierced mine as he looked intently at me with his head just above my face, "I have been so bitter and angry with all of this and I'm so ashamed," he paused to sort out his thoughts. "I know you've been praying for me and I've been praying too. God has touched my heart and it's starting to open. I can't believe what a jerk I've been. I didn't know how to process everything and I was scared, but God has worked everything out so far, right down to the smallest detail. Will you forgive me?"

I did my best not to blink as my eyes welled up with tears and I tried to push the knot in my throat further toward my stomach so that I could answer my husband's melodious question. He had just spoken the exact words, and *more,* that I had been praying so earnestly for, but thought would never come. I had seen his gradual shift in mood over the past few weeks, but this was as if he'd been living under a spell, and all of a sudden the spell had lifted and he was himself again, the man that I married almost four years earlier.

I was finally able to breathe out the words, "Yes, of course, Calv," using my favorite nickname. The moment was almost magical. Of course, I know it wasn't actually magic but the presence of the Holy Spirit that flooded the room at that moment as our hearts intertwined on a spiritual level. Nothing could take us down now. God had united us with threads that could not be broken, a bond that would last until our final days of life. An energy and feeling of supernatural strength filled me at that moment as I knew beyond a shadow of a doubt that our marriage would last, our baby was going to live, and our awesome God was going to be glorified through all of it.

Calvin's words obviously made it easier to approach him about my desire to pick a name for our little girl. His response was just as open as his apology had been: "Yeah Jen, it's time. We need to work on that. I'm sorry I was so closed off to it; I just didn't want to get too attached."

"I know," I paused for a moment while thoughts ran through my mind. "But like we've talked about before, God has just given me a belief that she's going to make it and I want to be ready."

"He's laid it on my heart too, Jen. I'm not sure how or why, but I believe she's going to make it too, and I want her. I can't wait to meet my precious girl."

His words sent me into another tear fest. I just couldn't stop the drops of water that spilled over the rims of my eyes. But this time, instead of being tears of sorrow, they were tears of joy. Oh the glorious difference between the two! One brought such feelings of angst and even deep-rooted depression, while the other brought elation and even glee. My God had done it again. He worked a miracle for little ol' me. Now, we were free to talk about baby names in a way that I had never imagined possible. Only through the awesome power of our God on high, Jesus!

8

Answered Prayer

As my heart calmed and my mind began to race at all the name possibilities, my mouth could hardly keep up. Names such as Nasia, meaning "gift of God," or Dasia, "miracle of Jehovah," were on the table just because of their meanings. But Nasia sounded too close to *nausea,* and many of the other names that we selected particularly for their meanings weren't really names that we liked. Other names, like Kalila, we considered because of its elegance and similarity to the genre of our older daughter's name, Ariana. But unlike Ariana's name, Kalila was Arabic and didn't have a profound meaning. We liked Ari's name because it is Hebrew, one of the languages that the Bible was originally written in, and the meaning is "holy song." How appropriate that our children's name meanings should portray our desire of how they'd appear before the Lord. That's what we wanted for the baby within me—that she'd have a lovely name, rich in godly heritage and deep with meaning.

Family names such as Breanne, Jane, and Grace were options because of the people they represented, but we liked those for middle names. Some names were cute and sweet just as we pictured our baby to be, like Claire and Kaitlyn, but the meanings were not what we were looking for. Our desire was that our little one would have a name that was all her own, a name that was not too common or too strange, and that fit her just right. One day, we came across a name that wouldn't let go of our attention. It seemed to have everything we were looking for. The sound of it as it rolled off the tongue was as sweet as a whisper, it's meaning, the exact symbol of what her life had been up to that point and what we hoped it would continue to be, and the origin was Greek, another language in which the Bible had been written. It was perfect.

"Shining brightly" was the meaning. Yes, already, this little baby had shined brightly to represent the glory of the Lord, and oh, if only she could go on shining for Him, that would be our greatest wish and desire. By living for Jesus and allowing Him to work through her life, we prayed that she would shine brightly to glorify Jesus. Pure and simple, simple and sweet, the name we chose for our little miracle baby was Ella.

Each week that passed, I'd receive a little certificate of achievement from the nursing staff at the hospital as a morale booster. It's amazing how you can start looking forward to little symbols of progress when your only goal is to lie in bed just to bring about the unlikely life of another human being. Keeping a positive outlook became more and more difficult as the possibility of her arrival neared. Having little to no fluid in the womb and being reminded of my baby's impossible chances each week at her ultrasound checks did not serve as a spirit booster either. And with the attacks of Satan's lies and depressive thoughts, I had to be in the Word of God for the majority of each day so that my mind would not devour my heart.

Already, my baby's life up to this point was nothing short of a miracle because she was surviving in the womb with basically no fluid. As long as my heart was pointed at the lamb, Jesus Christ, I had hope and perspective that did not allow me to wallow. People from church, as well as family, kept me busy with visits and messages that included perfect verses or poems that applied to what I was going through.

One visit I won't soon forget was from a dear friend, Laurie Haverfield. She took the 30-minute trip to the hospital and spent some time in prayer with me. Her prayer had been so powerful and reminded me of *who* was caring for my child: God Almighty! Before Laurie prayed, I had told her about some concerns that I was having. I thought I might not be shining for Jesus to the nurses and doctors in the midst of all the fear and doubt that the evil one had laid on my shoulders lately. Laurie responded by praying that God would post two of His warrior angels at my door so that no spirits of doubt, fear, anger or confusion would be able to enter, and that my room would be filled with only the peace, joy and light of Jesus. Oh, what a prayer! I clung to the words she spoke and proclaimed them in prayer over and over again after she left.

....

One thing that seemed odd to me during my stay at the hospital was that people who visited or called always seemed to vent or share what they were going through at that stage in their lives and yearned for wisdom and advice. At the time, I wondered why they had chosen to share their depressions with *me*, but as I would soon find out, God was working it all to His glory and my well-being and service to Him.

One phone call in particular, I received from a young girl in our youth group that I had been mentoring for a few years. "Jen, I'm not sure what to do!" Tina started in right after I answered the phone. "I slept with my boyfriend and I'm not sure if I'm pregnant, but now he's sleeping with someone else . . . What should I do?" she sobbed.

"Don't be so *stupid*!" I screamed at her inside my head, but I knew that wouldn't be very kind, or Christlike, so I thought for just a moment and prayed silently for the direction in which God would lead me to speak to this young girl that I loved so much.

"Sweet, sweet Tina, I'm so sorry," I started. I don't recall all of what I said, but when I got off the phone, I remember thinking, "Wow, where did those words come from?" It was especially odd that it had all flowed so gracefully since one of my nurse's assistants had been in the room and caused me to be a little distracted, but somehow, God had been incorporated in everything I said to her! I wondered what the nurse's assistant thought of the whole exchange, but knew that God had a plan for everything that was going on. Was it possible that my words could have touched the nurse's assistant in some way? I hoped so.

....

I always looked forward to craft day with the other moms on bed rest at the hospital. Today we were decorating bibs. I painted our newly chosen name, Ella, onto the fabric as I listened to the other moms chat. It was almost therapeutic to hear their stories and then to share my own account and have them completely understand. They could relate to the quirky nurse personalities, late-night cravings when the kitchen was closed, loneliness, and prison-like atmosphere of the hospital room. To have others that understood what I was going through was so important to me. Although none of them had quite the same situation as I had, it was still nice to be able to talk with other moms who were nervously anticipating the births of their children.

One mom, Christy, was pregnant with twins. Her water had broken at 22 weeks, so her babies had been blessed with a month's worth more fluid and lung development than our little Ella had. Another mom, Trista, was pregnant with one baby and had PROM as well (Premature Rupture of Membrane—her water broke) at 23 weeks and was still maintaining a good fluid level. Tammy, another mom, had gone into premature labor and suffered from high blood pressure, which initiated her hospital stay; she was also carrying twins. Of all the moms on bed rest in that hospital, my situation was by far the most high-risk, and being so, I had an amazing opportunity to share how God had comforted me as I journeyed to what seemed a fatal end for my baby and possibly myself.

Sitting around the craft table on one of the rare occasions I chose to sit upright, I noticed the demeanors and attitudes of each of the other women who joined me there. Each one had depressive thoughts and a hopeless attitude towards her situation. When I shared about how God had lifted my heart out of the pit and given me strength to endure everything, blank stares were directed my way. This strength and hope of Jesus was so foreign to them. When their conversation went on, I began to feel more and more out of the loop because we had less and less in common. Sarcasm, complaints, and defeat lined the words that were uttered around the table, and my only hope was that one of them might take hope in the words I had spoken that day.

....

The chances to share Jesus with others kept opening up and resulted in more touched lives than I could possibly imagine. One way that my story had spread was by e-mail. I kept my Grandpa Bob, the pastor, updated by e-mail since his hearing was failing, and he in turn forwarded my e-mails to countless others. I had no idea this was happening, but the stories of how my e-mails affected the people that read them were unbelievable. I don't know of every person my e-mails traveled to, but I do know that they reached as far east as Japan, as far south as the southern tip of South Africa, as far West as the Pacific Coast and Hawaii, and as far north as Alaska. I could have never imagined how my little e-mails to my grandpa would become so life-changing for so many individuals. Over and over I was told how my e-mails got someone thinking about their life. They thought if I could press on while lying in a bed with my baby dying each day, they could make it and create something beautiful with their lives and trust it to the hands of God Almighty. They'd then send my e-mail on to all of their friends, and so on and so on.

Originally, I wrote out a story of an experience I had while in the hospital to place at this point in the book, but just recently I deleted it because I found an old e-mail where I described it to my grandparents as I was encountering it. This e-mail was written April 29, 2008, ten and a half weeks after my water broke, while I was on bed rest at the hospital:

Dear Grandpa and Grandma,

I just thought I should share what God is doing here at the hospital. Right now, I am lying in bed, absolutely overwhelmed by God's power and glory. Sometimes I feel like it's just another day, and nothing significant is happening, but something that happened tonight woke me up to the fact that God is working in every moment. There have been so many wonderful miracles that have come from this situation so far, but I'd like to share two with you that happened this week.

Earlier this week, I had a young woman come and visit me with her mom. I had the best time talking with them. I think we talked for two hours! Eventually, they left and I went on with my week. A few days later, the young woman called me. I asked how she was doing, and a story unfolded. She told me about some things that she was dealing with and going through, and then, she told me that she was really glad that they had come to visit earlier that week because she was starting to think that there wasn't a God. That there wasn't really any reason or proof that He existed, but after our visit, she said that some things I had said had really made her think. We ended up talking for forty minutes that day on the phone. I was able to share some more examples of just the little things that God does for us every day, "mini-miracles."

When I got off of the phone, I was amazed at how God had used me that day that she and her mom had come to visit in the hospital. I had no idea that anything I was saying was actually sticking. It really woke me up to how God is so in control of this situation and every little thing going on because of it.

The second thing I wanted to share is a mini-story of one of the nurses' assistants that cares for me several times a week here at the hospital. Her name is Brenda. When she first came into my room, she was full of life and a very vibrant personality. God immediately laid her on my heart, and I began praying. One week after I'd been here, at the hospital, Brenda came into my room and said, "I have to tell you something. I just think it's really neat that you are so bold about your faith. I think that is so important." When Brenda said that, it kind of took me off guard. I told her "thank you," and then began trying to remember when I'd shared God with her…. I couldn't remember a single time. After considering this for quite some time, I realized that she'd been present when I'd been on the phone with a young girl from our church and was counseling her in what might be a godly reaction to her situation. And Brenda had also been there a few times that I had visitors and we were discussing what God was doing in my life. She must have been listening and we didn't even realize what was going on in her heart and mind.

Then, tonight (three weeks into my stay) Brenda started her shift and came in to see if I needed anything. I had a strong impression upon my heart that I needed to ask her how she was doing. So I said, "I remember you were sick last week, are you OK?" And she said, "Oh, yeah . . . you remember that? Wow, you have a good memory." Then, I felt I needed to specifically ask about her. So I asked, "Are you *alright tonight?" And she said, "Wow, you're in here, and you're worried about me. You are always so cheerful and wanting to know how we're doing. You're just so awesome."*

I didn't know what to say. Brenda then left to fill up my water. When she came back, she just started talking again and said, "You know, I've told you this before, but I just think it's so neat how you share your faith and are not afraid to do it. And I've been waiting for a chance to tell you this and keep forgetting, but when you first came to the hospital I felt like you had said a prayer for me. Something just told me that."

Then, my mind started reeling! How did she know? I had prayed for her that first night that God would use me and that she'd be saved. So I asked her, "How did you know?" She said, "Well, I don't know what you call it, the Spirit or something, told me. I just knew."

I just about started crying. God was moving in ways that I could never have imagined. He is so much BIGGER than I ever give Him credit for. I didn't even have to open my mouth directly to her and speak about Jesus, He was shining through me the whole time, and I didn't even know it. I am so excited to see what else He has planned for Brenda. I've got six more weeks here if all goes well, and I know it will. Would you pray for Brenda?

What an amazing God we serve! I've found myself saying that a LOT lately.

Praise Jesus! Glory halleluiah! All praise and glory goes to Him, the one who created the earth. The great I Am.

I just thought you should know. I love you Grandpa and Grandma.

Love, Jen

9

Faith

Just two days after meeting with the moms at the group craft time, I learned from one of the nurses that Trista, one of the ladies whose water had broken early (much later than mine at 23 weeks) had gone into irreversible labor the night before and delivered her baby. I did not find out through the nurse what the outcome was (because of privacy laws), but through a strange series of people bumping into other people, the story was relayed to me by my parents.

Trista had gone into labor that the doctors said could not be stopped, so her baby boy was born early. Being 25 weeks and having sufficient fluid, her baby should have had a fairly good chance at surviving, but a severe brain-bleed killed him in his first seconds of life. Being 28 weeks pregnant myself, it hit close to home. I knew that Ella had no chances of surviving according to the doctors and the thing that would most likely prove fatal for her would be her undeveloped lungs. The peace and calm I had been riding on was suddenly pulled out from under me as worry and fear began to creep in.

Trista had what seemed to be gallons more amniotic fluid than I had in the course of my entire pregnancy, and her baby died! It didn't matter that my baby was making it weeks longer, because Ella's organs were not developing. Was I setting myself up for heartbreak? Then, God whispered His promise into my heart, *"Your baby is going to live."*

"But why?" my thoughts erupted angrily. "Why will my baby live and not hers?" I wondered as passion and sorrow pulsed through my body. "How can God choose one to live and another to die?" The thoughts surged on. This question of how and why God chooses good for some people and allows sorrow and tragedy to affect others flooded my heart and mind. For days this question loomed over me, and my struggle to stay positive became more intense.

But just as God had always been faithful to me, He gave me a verse that revealed an acceptable answer to my dilemma. 2 Timothy 2:10 says, "So I patiently accept all these troubles so that those whom God has chosen can have the salvation that is in Christ Jesus. With that salvation comes glory that never ends" (NCV). You may wonder how that verse answered my questions, and I will explain it to you. God does everything in order that His glory may be seen. Not because He is an arrogant, egotistical God who wants everyone to see Him and worship Him, but because He is "not wanting anyone to perish" (2 Peter 3:9).He wants people to see His glory so that they may come to Him and receive eternal life!

I guess I began to understand that God can see above the fog of each situation and can distinguish how He will be glorified most, causing people to be saved from eternal suffering. No situation or precious life passes through this world without God allowing it. I wasn't going through all of this for nothing, and neither did Trista. It was as I had always thought it to be from the very first moment God asked me if I'd use this situation for His glory in my closet . . . His desire was to bring others to Him!

My faith had been given a brutal blow when Trista's baby died, but was mended with the amazing love and grace of my Lord and Savior, Jesus Christ. He *died* first so that we don't have to. There is not a more sacrificial example of love and grace than that of Jesus on the cross. "For God so loved the world that he gave his one and only Son, that whoever believes in him shall not perish but have eternal life" (John 3:16). Now *that* is passionate love. Our God is not just up there zapping us and cursing people as they live their lives. No, He is there as we stumble, to gently lift us to our feet, wipe our tears, and lead us to His saving grace as we look to Him in all of our needs and trials.

....

As I slid out of my hospital bed and quickly walked toward the wheelchair that awaited me, I wondered what I would see in the minutes that would follow. Calvin and Ariana had come to take me on a walk to visit the Newborn Intensive Care Unit (NICU) to prepare for what might be our new "home" if Ella made it even for a few hours. My doctor had not recommended the visit, as he was adamant that my baby would not be born alive, but the nursing staff thought it might be a good little outing for me, even if it was just down the hall.

Once inside the NICU, one of the nurses took us on a mini-tour of the unit and let us peer into the windows to view some of the critical babies that they were caring for. I was not prepared for what I saw. Tiny little human beings lay, seemingly lifeless, on miniature hospital beds with tubes and wires flowing into their bodies, sustaining them seconds at a time. Not all of them were premature. Some were normal-sized babies that were dealing with life-threatening illnesses; others could not maintain their own temperatures and were inside of incubators, while others, called micro preemies (babies born at 24 weeks gestation), only the length of a writing pen, fought for life on a flat-exposed bed that warmed their bodies with an overhead light while tubes and machines worked to keep their little bodies running.

I'll never forget the moment that the "tour guide nurse" held out a petite diaper to show me what the smallest babies wore. "Your baby will probably not need one this small if it stays in your tummy for much longer," she guessed as she held out the tiny specimen that fit completely within the palm of her hand. I just stared at the tiny diaper and tried to imagine how big our little babe was at that very moment. Could she wear such a miniscule diaper?

Our trip to the NICU had opened my eyes to what I needed to prepare myself for. I knew that God was promising me that our baby would live, but I never really thought about what her life would look like. Even if Ella made it to 34 weeks, the maximum the doctors would allow me to progress, she would have to be hospitalized until she met certain criteria that would allow her to go home.

Also, while in the NICU, we met with a neonatologist, which is just a fancy name for a baby doctor with specialized skills. Dr. Zara was his name, and we decided right away that we liked him very much. His thick Middle-Eastern accent was hard to understand, but his black eyes sparkled as he spoke, giving us insight into his kind personality. The news he had for us, however, was not uplifting or new. After looking over my pregnancy history, he confirmed what we'd been told all along by Dr. Striker. Ella was in a very dangerous position.

At this point, she was breech, had little to no fluid, was not developing her lungs, and her bones were being crushed by the weight of my uterus, which is the hardest muscle in the body. His prediction was that even if Ella miraculously gained use of her lungs, she'd be doomed to a life of reconstructive surgeries and confined to full-body casts as doctors worked to straighten her bent and twisted bones that were crushed in the womb. These curvatures are called bone contractures, and he predicted that Ella would have many. The news was a bit disheartening, but then again, it wasn't any different than we'd been hearing all along.

Through each tidbit of new information, the peace that surpasses all understanding was a constant companion, along with the knowledge that the doctors are not God! I did not believe, after all, that Ella was actually in my womb . . . I mean, of course she was in there, but I believed that God was holding her in His mighty and completely capable hands! What's the point of believing *in* God if you don't actually believe in His promises and that He will do what He says He will do?

While on Earth, Jesus Himself promised us this in Mark 11:22-24, "'Have faith in God,' Jesus answered. 'I tell you the truth, if anyone says to this mountain, "Go, throw yourself into the sea," and does not doubt in his heart but believes that what he says will happen, it will be done for him. Therefore I tell you, whatever you ask for in prayer, believe that you have received it, and it will be yours.'"

....

Once back in my hospital room, my thoughts were interrupted by the entrance of one of the maternal fetal medicine docs doing rounds. His name was Dr. Blake; he was my favorite. The words that he uttered were always positive, no matter the circumstance. Today, as he checked me he chatted about how neat it had been to see Ella having the hiccups on the ultrasound earlier in the week, and how wonderful it was to be in the "happy room" with me. "You know, now we just need your little baby to turn so that her little bottom doesn't want to come out first," he said as he examined my slowly growing tummy. "Can she turn even without fluid?" I asked curiously. "Sure!" he said without missing a beat and with a twinkle in his eye. I loved this doctor; he never mentioned the impossibility of my pregnancy and always tried to be uplifting. It was my deepest hope that he'd be on duty when I went into labor so that he could deliver Ella. There was a one in four chance that he'd be the one to do it because there were four MFM doctors that rotated caring for the women on Antepartum. Given all the time I had to just lie in bed, I had all four MFM doctors rated and scored in the order of how much I liked them. Dr. Blake, of course, was at the top of my list.

"Well, 29 weeks!" he congratulated me. "If we can get to 30, your baby's chance of a brain bleed goes down significantly," he said optimistically as he looked down at his notes and finished up his visit. "Let's make it to that mark, OK?" he grinned as he stepped out of my room.

....

Little flutters of movement in my abdomen always jolted to a halt whatever I was doing and brought my attention fully to the baby that continued to live within me. Because my fluid was so low, Ella had very little space to move around in as the walls of my uterus closed in around her, but when she did move, I cherished each little poke and stretch. Having the unusual event of movement in my stomach sent my mind back to 16 weeks of pregnancy in a moment of sweet ignorance while I enjoyed a nice warm bath, when all of a sudden, the baby within me started moving and rolling, punching and jabbing so much so that I could see the movement from the outside of my very small, early-pregnancy stomach. I just sat there and enjoyed the glorious sight of my tummy dancing with delight as the very tiny person within me exercised her ability to move. That was the last time I had felt my little baby, Ella, move with such freedom and enjoyment of *space*.

When I had mentioned my bathtub experience to the nurses that were caring for me in the hospital, many of them joked that Ella had kicked a hole in her own sac! Others amazingly stated that she had been a fighter right from the beginning, but whatever the case, that time in the bathtub was sweet and a cherished memory. As my mind flashed back to the moment I was currently experiencing on my hospital bed with the little pokes and long stretches that came from within my midsection, I was overwhelmed with the blessing of my unborn daughter's little life! What a blessing and what a miracle! I had now made it 11 weeks on bed rest with no signs of infection.

....

May 7, 2008 started out like any other day in the hospital, full of reading, Sudoku, meals and the occasional visitor (including Calvin), but it did not end in the same way as all the rest. At three o'clock in the afternoon, I began having painful contractions. The entire time I had been on bed rest at home and in the hospital, I had experienced frequent and often painful contractions, but these were different, somewhat closer together and progressing in strength. At first, I thought nothing of them as they had been occurring all along, but as the pain heightened, I began to wonder if there might be something to these strange contractions. Finally after about an hour of very strong and steady contractions, I buzzed my nurse, Leslie, to let her know that this afternoon's monitoring session might need to come a bit sooner than usual.

After half an hour on the monitor, it was clear that my contractions were not only strong and consistent, but showed signs of real labor. Nurse Leslie paged the doctor on call, who happened to be my favorite doctor, Dr. Blake. His instructions were to inject into my arm a drug called terbutaline that would hopefully stop labor from occurring at this early stage in pregnancy. My goal was to make it to 34 weeks, the farthest they'd allow me. If the baby was born at this point, I'd only be 29 weeks and 6 days gestation, one day short of even the 30 week mark.

I could tell the medicine was kicking in when my contractions started to soften and my body began trembling, a side effect of the medication. For about 30 minutes I thought we had bypassed the scare of early delivery. That is, until the contractions came back, and this time, they were stronger.

10

Labor and Delivery

AFTER BEING ON BED REST for almost 12 weeks, I was used to these up and down spikes and was not too alarmed by the contractions I was experiencing. Even after two pills were given to me and another shot of terbutaline administered, I hadn't thought at any length about Ella being born that night. It wasn't until my nurse, Leslie, made a comment to me that I really started contemplating my situation. "Don't you think you ought to call Cal?" she quizzed. "Really? You think it's *that* likely that our baby will be born tonight . . . " I trailed off as my mind tried to understand what an early delivery could mean for our sweet Ella. "Honey, you're in labor. If I was in labor, you better believe I wouldn't be doing it alone," she said with a knowing look. Leslie finished repositioning the monitors that were strapped around my torso and then left to get a second dose of the labor-delaying medication.

Without delay, I picked up the phone and dialed the familiar number to Cal's cell phone. "Hello?" came the deep voice on the other end. "Calv, it's Jen . . . " I let the line hang silent for a moment as I searched for words. "Can you come to the hospital?" I questioned. "I was just there earlier; are you OK? Is everything OK?" his voice sounded concerned. "Yeah, everything's fine. It's just that . . . I might be going into labor and the nurse thought," I paused, feeling somewhat guilty asking more of him than was already required. But after realizing that he needed to be there for the birth of his daughter, I gained more steam, continued and corrected myself, " *I* thought you'd want to come and be with me in case Ella is born tonight," I said with resolve. "Soooo, you *might* be in labor?" Cal responded slowly, seemingly trying to better understand the situation. "Well, I've got some pretty strong contractions. They gave me a few shots to try and stop them, but they're still coming. I mean, I've had this shot in the past and the contractions stopped right away and these ones are still coming." I waited to hear his decision.

"Let me give Ari some dinner and put her to bed. I'll get over there as soon as I can. Love you, Jen," he said as I could tell he was mentally processing everything that needed to be done. "I love you too," I whispered. As we hung up the phone I knew that he was worried that if this was a false alarm, he'd still be on his very regimented schedule, starting his day at midnight . . . but would have to do it all on little to no sleep. Shortly after my phone call with Cal had ended, my contractions started to spike more sharply than before.

....

Cal arrived at 8:15 p.m., just as the nurses were packing up my home of nearly five weeks and moving me to a bed on the labor and delivery unit of the hospital. There we stayed and watched my contractions progress on a monitor for three hours. A nurse came and gave us operating room attire to change into to prepare for an emergency C-section, just in case. Doctor Blake came in to see how I was progressing and said, "If we can wait any longer at all, I want to. I'd like to get you past midnight and into your 30th week. If we can hold off for a bit, your baby will have significantly higher chances of having less developmental problems and almost zero chance of brain hemorrhage." It sounded good to me, so we prepared to wait a little bit longer.

A little after midnight, on May 8, 2008, my bed was wheeled next door to a room where they would remove my baby from the womb in an emergency C-section and God's love would be revealed.

Even though I knew that Ella's chance of survival was less than if she were a normal baby at 24 weeks gestation (the age of viability) because she hadn't had any fluid to develop her organs, I could feel Jesus' overwhelming presence with me; it was almost euphoric. The doctors probably thought I was in denial when I came in with all smiles and greeted each of them with joy. And I was not the only one. This time, Calvin shared in my complete joy and peace. There was no anger, there were no silent moments of sorrow, for we were both entirely joyful in this beautiful moment while we awaited the birth of our daughter. Even though she was coming earlier than we had hoped, it was sort of an ideal situation since my body naturally went into labor and was not induced by doctors because of a supposed infection or other medical issue. God had even allowed for our favorite doctor to deliver our baby. Dr. Blake, "the optimistic one," as we called him, would introduce our tiny babe to this world. What a blessing.

As the final preparations were finished for my C-section and the doctors started to cut, I got very excited and asked Calvin to take some photos. Looking back at Calvin, and noticing the sickening color of green he was turning, my anesthesiologist ordered Calvin to put the camera down and sit on the floor. Calvin had had a hard time during the birth of our first daughter as well, but the thought of the doctors cutting me open apparently was more than Cal could stomach, and he was on the verge of passing out. So, my wonderful anesthesiologist took the photos as my doctors worked.

I remember feeling pressure in my abdomen as the doctors cut layer after layer of skin and muscle to reach our baby who lay within. The oddest part was when both doctors took hold of my skin and muscle on their individual sides and began pulling back with all their might so as to open the wound to expose our girl. From my view behind the little curtain that hung between my face and belly, I could see the doctors above the division, and it looked as if my stomach would split and they'd be sent flying backwards with the force of their pulling. Of course, my skin stayed intact and they reached the object of their hunt, Ella.

All of a sudden I was aware that they were no longer working on me, and their attention was focused on something else at the foot of my bed. The mysterious object of their attention, our precious little baby, was whisked to a table to the side of my operating table, and a flurry of doctors, neonatologist, nurses and respiratory therapists swarmed the little table to work on her as my doctor resumed work on me.

I had no idea what was going on. The room was completely silent as everyone worked diligently. There had been no quick showing of my baby, no sounds of congratulations on a beautiful baby girl, no looks of joy or accomplishment, and no cry of a newborn baby. Silence was the only present sense, and it was deafening. As I watched the medical staff who were crowded around my baby, I prayed. Not a prayer for help, but a prayer of thanksgiving. My heart could not feel worry. It was impossible. I did not feel helpless or fearful. Joy was my only companion as I curiously kept my eyes locked on the table to my left. My heart was full with the hope and peace that came from Jesus Christ, my Lord and Savior! And in a moment of pure elation, I interrupted the silence with the announcement of her name, "This is Ella Breanne Wilkins!" The announcement came a little too loudly because of the loss of hearing I was experiencing from the medication. Immediately, my doctor's sad eyes met mine and locked for just a moment before he looked back to his work of sewing me up. I didn't mind that he probably thought I was nuts, I just knew that God was working and His presence was flooding that operating room and filling me with a sweeping sense of peace and absolute glee!

As I peered over at the table where my tiny baby lay with several medical people surrounding her, at one point there was a sliver of visibility between two doctors, and I saw the tiniest little arm shoot up into the air and fall back down. Was that a sign of life? I had no way of telling from my point of view if it had been a natural movement or not, but I did know that it was the miniature arm of my newborn daughter. In the split second that I could see it, her little arm looked pretty normal other than the fact that it was incredibly small and her hand seemed to be cocked off to the right a bit, which I assumed to be one of many bone-contractures that we'd been warned about. But nothing could break my joy, not even the undetermined status of her life. My eyes continued to try and blaze through the doctors that stood between me and my daughter, but I had no luck; in an instant, my baby girl was whisked out of the room, followed directly by her daddy. I could feel my heart trailing them, but even though my body lingered, I did not feel alone.

....

As I lay in the recovery room, my head spun with wonder at what could possibly be happening with my baby at that moment. Had she lived? How much did she weigh? I knew that we'd be very lucky if she weighed two pounds at 30 weeks, but really, I would take anything. Waiting was hard; all I wanted to do was jump out of bed and run to Ella's bedside to gawk at the creation God had given to us, but I was told that I would be unable to see Ella until my spinal block wore off enough that I could pull my legs up and wiggle my toes. I remember lying there, willing my toes to move, but nothing would happen. What torture to not be with my new baby! To not have even been allowed a glimpse! I didn't even know if she was alive, or if she *was* alive, how long her little life would last! What did she look like? Was she bald like her sister had been? Whose features did she have? Ariana was the spitting image of Calvin, so maybe Ella would look like me. Would she have blue eyes, or maybe brown like her daddy? There were so many curious wonderments that consumed my being, but most of all, I just wanted to know if she had made it!

As the thoughts continued to tumble around in my head, shooting pain that stabbed like a knife cutting into a thick piece of meat engulfed my neck. I could hardly breathe it was so intense. The nurse informed me that it was something called "referred pain." Apparently, sometimes a person can experience excruciating pain in the neck or shoulders when senses are cut off to the lower part of the body that is experiencing severe trauma; it sort of refers it upward. After the stabbing sensation died down a bit, my face, right under my nose, began to itch profusely and I was thirsty beyond description of words! The nurse refused to give me water because of the spinal block and my having just undergone surgery, so she got me ice. I wish I could have been a fly on that wall watching me scarf down ice chips in record time and ask for more time and time again.

In the midst of all my ice munching, the phone rang next to my bed. No one was in the room, so I answered. It was my life-long friend, Brittany. She worked at the hospital as a respiratory therapist and happened to be working that night. "Jen!" she exclaimed excitedly. "Hey Britt! I had my baby . . . I don't know anything yet, but I just had her," I sputtered, a little frustrated that I didn't have much news to share. "Well, that's why I'm calling," her voice almost sang with joy, "Jen, Ella's alive and she weighs three pounds!" she almost shouted.

Immediately my heart stopped. She was *alive*! Adrenaline kicked in and I could not sit still. If it were not for my Jello-legs, those nurses would have never been able to keep me in bed. Oh, how the emotion flooded right to the center of my very being! "She is *alive*! My baby's alive!" I wanted to scream. I don't even remember the rest of the phone call because of the elation I was experiencing. I do remember, however, singing. I sang a hymn and let it ring out loud and clear, "I love you, Lord," I started out, "And I lift my voice, to worship you, oh my soul . . . *rejoice*!" At that moment, my Labor and Delivery nurse walked in, looked at me, and walked right back out. She must've thought they had my medication cranked too high or that I was going crazy, because I was singing up a storm with tears streaming down my face and hands lifted to the Lord in praise—but I didn't care! My baby was *alive* and I was ecstatic! Praise Him! Praise the One who *is* and who *was* and who is *yet* to come! The *great I Am*! *King of kings and Lord of lords, Almighty God! To Him be the glory forever and ever*!

....

Soft dark wisps of hair encircled her sweet little face. She was so tiny and frail. I'd never seen anything like her. As I was allowed a peek at my tiny daughter from my hospital bed that they'd rolled down to the NICU, I couldn't help but notice the extensive number of cords and tubes that were inserted into her miniature body just to keep her going. She wasn't quite as small as some of the other babies I had seen, but close. They told me she was only 15 inches long, but now that I looked at her, she didn't even look that long. I noticed she was wearing one of those tiny diapers I had been shown only a few days earlier. "I guess she didn't cook long enough," I thought, referring to my pregnancy and her petite size. My eyes wanted to examine every inch of her, but the medical staff who were assisting me didn't allow me to get out of bed, and because Ella's bed was too high to allow a good view from where I was lying, I didn't get the examination I was hoping for.

One picture that was completely satisfying was watching my husband adore his new daughter. He just bent over her open bed looking down at her with complete awe. He kept saying over and over to his precious babe, "I just want to hold you. I love you." The sight was so moving. I'll never forget it as long as I live.

When my few minutes was up with Ella and the hospital staff rolled me out of her hospital room, I felt as if my heart would literally come ripping out of my chest to stay near her. What an unnatural thing to be separated from my new baby! As I was rolled down the hall and away from my husband and daughter, I reflected on the fact that she was *alive*! Just that one piece of information would keep me going through the night.

11

Life Support

I WAS TOLD THAT MY recovery would be longer and more extensive because my C-section was not performed on a fully-expanded tummy, so the amount of skin and muscle that they cut through was significantly more than usual. I was going to be bed-bound at least until morning. Trying to sleep that night was impossible. All I wanted to do was look at my girl, to hold her and nurse her. I can't say that my night apart from my darling daughter was easy because of the joy of the Lord. Fear and frustration did creep in and grab hold of me for a few moments when thoughts like, "What if she dies before I get to see her again?" or "What if they move her and forget who she belongs to?" entangled my mind, until I was able to see that the evil one was trying to make his mark on our night of miracle. I then put a stop to that line of thinking and closed the door on Satan and his evil schemes and lies.

I did ask the nurse for my pump so that I could try to encourage my breast milk to come in, even though I hadn't made it full-term. Just doing that small action of pumping milk for my tiny baby gave me a sense of participation in her care. Even though she wouldn't be able to use the milk for days to come because of her premature state, I knew I needed to start in order to get a supply started. Once finished, I tried to rest, but sleep evaded me. The thought that my baby had been born and was only a hallway away sent excitement pulsing through my veins and kept my eyes from closing. As the adrenaline surged, I reveled in the miracle of Ella's birth, and now her *life,* as time slowly clicked by until finally morning came.

....

With the early light of dawn came my intense desire to see my baby daughter. Calvin had come to care for me during the night and was with me as the first rays of sunshine peeked around the curtains and into my new room at the hospital. Nothing much was said, since both Cal and I were exhausted from the long night of waiting. The first thing I did was hit the call button for my nurse to come in to see if I could make a trip down to the NICU.

After a few very painful attempts and one successful scoot and upward motion with the help of the strong arms of Calvin and my nurse, I was able to stand and take the two excruciating steps it took to get into the wheelchair. "It's best to stay seated," my nurse instructed. "It might cause some bleeding if you overdo it." I assured her that we would be fine as Cal rolled me out the door.

Our mini-trip to the NICU seemed endless as the halls just kept going on and on. Loud thumps drummed ferociously within my chest as my excitement peaked. I could hardly stand the next few steps it would take to get to my new little baby. I longed for a closer look at her.

Finally we reached two electronic doors that could only be opened by the person at the desk inside. We used a phone hung on the wall just adjacent to the tightly closed doors to announce our presence and gain permission to enter the NICU. After arriving inside, we were required to "scrub in." The washroom held sinks from one wall to the other that were controlled by foot pedals so as not to spread germs. An entire set of hand-washing instructions hung on the wall, covering every conceivable rule about hand washing. Once we were thoroughly cleaned, Calvin took me to my girl.

As my wheelchair rolled into Ella's hospital room, I realized immediately that I was not going to be able to obey my nurse's orders to stay seated. Ella's bed was too high and blocked my view from my position in the chair. With Calvin's help, I struggled to a standing position. The pain and effort it took to stand up had been worth it. My tiny baby girl was a fascinating sight. I had never seen anything like her; she was my baby, all right. I recognized her Miller (my maiden name) feet right off the bat: wide, with toes that were thick and pudgy in comparison with the rest of her miniature body. They *had* to be Miller feet!

It was hard to see if there was any family resemblance in her face, because her nose and mouth were contorted by the obnoxious tubes and wires feeding into them. Her hands and eyes were the only places on her body that seemed to have any fat, and even that was actually just swelling. Her skin was so transparent you could see every hair-thin vein that ran through her body. Ella's skull was incredibly narrow due to lack of fluid in my womb; it looked as if she had stuck her head sideways in a waffle iron because it was so narrow. We found out later that nurses had a name of their own for heads that were shaped like Ella's—"Toaster Head," they called it.

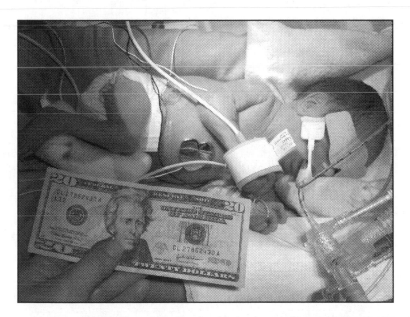

This is Ella the way she looked when I first saw her

Tiny tubes and wires surrounded Ella's tiny body and led into several different locations. Two miniscule wires fed through the hole in her belly button, carrying medication and nutrients directly into her veins. Another little line ran along her torso and threaded into a heart-shaped sticky monitor that read Ella's temperature and controlled the thermostat of her bed. Several small plastic cup-like pieces were stuck randomly on her body; I found out later they were used to test the iron in her body. Ella also wore a blood pressure cuff and a Band-Aid like sticker that read the oxygen levels in her blood, but perhaps the most intrusive and unsightly device on her body was the enormous tube that fed into Ella's mouth to supply oxygen directly to her underdeveloped lungs. Accompanying the large tube was a tiny hose that ran into Ella's nose, down her throat, and into her stomach.

Loud swirling and pumping sounds were coming from the machines surrounding Ella's bed. With all the noises and sparkling machines, there was almost too much to take in. As my eyes surveyed my precious child and all of the medical equipment keeping her alive, an eerie feeling swept over me. Ella wasn't moving. Her eyes were not open and she didn't even look like she was breathing. She looked dead. What was wrong? Immediately I turned to Ella's nurse who was standing right next to Ella's bed, monitoring her every second. "Why is she so still?" I asked, trying not to sound panicked.

"We've sedated her completely," the nurse, Candice, started. "Her little body could not function on its own and so when they're born so premature like this, we sedate them so that they don't work too hard and burn too many calories. These little ones actually burn more calories just trying to breathe than they take in during a day," she informed me. "She does have a brain bleed; the doctors did an X-ray during the night and are having a neurologist look at it." She casually flipped through her notes and continued, "We should have some results for you later on today or tomorrow." The words brought my universe to a halt. I'm not sure if Candice was unaware of our shock or if she was used to being the deliverer of bad news, but I felt as if my heart had dropped to my stomach, and she had just announced it like it was as normal as taking out the trash. What did she mean, Ella had a brain bleed? I mean, I know what she meant, but it just didn't seem real.

Dr. Blake had said that there was almost no chance of having a brain bleed after 30 weeks gestation. Ella had barely made the 30 week mark by being born at 1:27 a.m., but she *had* made it. Maybe Ella was at a higher risk because of my lack of fluid.

New ideas and concepts started attacking me. "Is Ella going to die? This is how Trista's baby died while I was on bed rest. If Ella lives, will she ever be able to function as a normal person? Is she going to have cerebral palsy?" Without missing a beat, the questions continued to torment, but I could not bring myself to ask them aloud. I'm not sure why I couldn't ask; it may have been because I was afraid of what Candice would think of me for asking selfish questions like, "Is she going to be mentally challenged?" Or it may have been because I was afraid of her answers, but whatever the reason, I did not voice even one.

"Do you want to touch her?" came the unexpected question from Candice. After a brief moment of uncertainty, I whispered, "Can I?"

"Yes; you won't be able to hold her because she's too frail, and on the ventilator it's just too risky, but you can place your hands like this," Candice demonstrated by placing one hand around the curve of Ella's small bottom and the other hand on the top of Ella's head. "You just place your hands here and create a safe boundary for her. It's tight, like the womb. Don't rub her skin or squeeze her just yet because her sensory system can't handle the input and her skin is too fragile to handle the friction." Noticing the trepidation on my face, Candice encouraged me, "Try not to worry too much, though, just enjoy your baby."

I placed my hands on my miniature baby for the first time; my right hand, on her head and my left, on her little bum. There was not even 10 inches of space between my two hands. How crazy to think that a tiny little person lay in a seven- or eight-inch distance! I let my hands rest on my precious daughter for several minutes until I thought to ask Cal if he wanted a turn. He didn't even hesitate; as he placed his large hands around the body of his premature baby, she almost disappeared in the mass of them. Cal leaned his face near Ella's and began whispering to her. I didn't hear all of what he said, but the few words I did hear were, "I love you Ella. Jesus gave you to us and I can't wait to hold you."

At that moment I knew I had been blessed with two miracles: the first, my husband's changed heart and mind, and the second, the life of my new little baby daughter. Once we became a bit more comfortable with our surroundings, Candice began telling us all about Ella and how she was being kept alive. "The ventilator that is breathing for Ella right now is called the 'jet.' They call it that because it pushes rapid puffs of oxygen in at such a quick pace so that it doesn't pop her tiny lung pockets," she informed us as she seemed to be searching her mind and Ella's chart for more tidbits of information. Then she continued, "Ella actually didn't give us much to work with last night when she was born. We shot a medication called surfactant into her lungs to lubricate them so the first puff of air would be able to squeeze in and open them up."

Then, Candice turned to me and gave me the strangest look, as if her eyes were trying to penetrate right into my soul. "You know," she started, "you are incredibly lucky. Last night when your daughter was born, she scored zero on her Apgar score. Do you know what that is?" she questioned. "No, I don't know," I answered, but felt anxious to find out. "The Apgar score is based on how well or poorly a baby is doing at birth. Doctors use it to assess several different areas of life such as responsiveness, heart rate, breathing, and skin color in newborn babies. They rate the baby anywhere from zero, which is no signs of life, to ten, which is healthy and active. When Ella was born, she had no pulse, was unable to breathe, was blue in color, and was completely lifeless.

"Five minutes later, after intubation and lots of work, she scored a 5, and at 10 minutes of life, they had resuscitated her enough that she scored a 9, and they were able to transport her to the NICU. You almost didn't get her, and truth be told," Candice said with a sigh, "every second she is alive now is a lucky one. She may not have long," she said as gently as possible.

I was completely speechless. Short, quick breaths passed through my lips, and I felt as though I couldn't suck in any oxygen. Tears welled up in my eyes, and I turned my gaze back to my lifeless daughter and looked her over for several seconds before lifting my eyes to my precious husband who stood quietly at my side supporting my arm so that I would not fall. Tears threatened to spill over his eye lids as he gave me a look of pure peace and deep amazement at the gift that God had given us. No words needed to be spoken, for we both knew the miracle that had taken place in the life of our little Ella. A precious secret lay in our hearts at that moment;

it was that Cal and I both knew beyond a shadow of a doubt what Ella's outcome would be— *life*!

Questions started to pound around inside my head and as I was about to let one escape, I felt a gush of fluid between my legs. When my eyes scanned past my hospital gown and made it to the floor, I realized blood had started to spill out and around the catheter that I had not been patient enough for the nurse to remove before coming to see my girl. As soon as Candice noticed what was going on, she ordered me back into the wheelchair and to my room to rest.

Not only was I completely embarrassed and humiliated, but I was frustrated as well! A miracle had just been given me and I could not even enjoy her! There were so many questions I wanted to ask, so many pictures I wanted to take, and so many more moments of just staring at Ella I wanted to have; returning to my room because my body was not cooperating was the last thing I wanted to do.

As I tried to come to terms with my sentencing, I prayed that God would hold our little babe, that He would keep her and sustain her little life so that I could see her again!

12

Bad News

QUIET MOMENTS WITH JESUS WERE all that kept my heart beating during the first day and a half of Ella's life, as new realizations and worries flooded my already-full mind. With the blessing of Ella's life came new uncertainties and reservations. "What if I have gone through all of these weeks of waiting and separation from Cal and Ariana only for Ella to die?" my psyche tormented. "And how much longer is Ella going to be in the hospital if she lives? I don't think I can go one more day without going home to my precious Ariana!" But as soon as that whisper came to my mind, I felt guilty for even considering being away from Ella.

As the thoughts rushed on, the knot in my throat ascended until I could hardly breathe. "*Calm,*" God's familiar voice spoke to my heart. "*Trust me. You will make it, even if I have to carry you,*" I felt Him whisper to my soul.

Through each new trial, fear, worry or doubt, Jesus was right there with me. His presence and never-ending blessings were as a healing balm on my torn and tattered heart. In my hospital room during one of the many mandatory rest times after my C-section, I decided to spend some time with Jesus. As I cracked open my Bible and sifted through the well-used pages, my finger rested on a page in Hebrews. I began reading at the start of chapter 12:

"Therefore, since we are surrounded by such a great cloud of witnesses," it read, "let us throw off everything that hinders and the sin that so easily entangles, and let us run with perseverance the race marked out for us. Let us fix our eyes on Jesus, the author and perfecter of our faith, who for the joy set before him endured the cross, scorning its shame, and sat down at the right hand of the throne of God. Consider him who endured such opposition from sinful men, so that you will not grow weary and lose heart."

Fix our eyes on Jesus, I echoed in my mind. "Oh Jesus, help me to fix my eyes on you, that I will only see with eternal eyes and not these human ones that so frequently despair at the first sign of trouble. Help my precious Ella to be OK, to grow and thrive, and sustain my little Ariana through the rest of the time I have to be away from her. Keep me strong and able to endure what lies ahead," I cried out to my best friend and Savior.

Even after reading God's word that day, a heavy weight hung in my chest at the thought of more time away from my one-and-a half-year old at home. I had already missed so many of her momentous milestones while I was on bed rest for three months; could *I* endure another second away? The answer was most certainly no. That emotion collided with the love I had for my new baby. How could I choose between the two? I couldn't do it. "Will Ari think that I am picking Ella over her if I stay with Ella?"

Irrational thoughts attacked me from every direction, "Will Ari remember me if I'm gone longer and only see her once a week? I will just be like a day care worker to her . . . " Guilt and fear clouded everything. "But if I leave Ella, she'll be all alone. I can't leave her. She'll have no one. The only person she knows is me; my voice was the only one that was with her every day before her birth. I *cannot* leave her," my heart screamed. The thought of separating from Ella was as unnatural as peeling a scab from a new wound. Deep sobs overtook me as my mind fought an impossible battle over my two children. This is how Calvin found me, in a heap on my hospital bed, hair and tears intertwined and covering my face.

In one swift motion he was beside me, placing his large arms around my body. He quietly held me as I wept intensely for what seemed like 10 minutes. He did not say a word, just held me tenderly as the hurt, pain, frustration, anger, and sorrow flowed from the deepest corners of my being. Finally, when there were no more tears to cry, I turned to him and asked, "What am I going to do?" After his eyes scanned every detail of my face, a hint of a smile snuck onto Calvin's lips. "What do you mean?" he questioned. "How am I going to take care of Ari and still be here for Ella?" I said. The words barely made it out of my mouth before new tears and sobs burst out and took me back to the puddle I had been before.

A kind and caring chuckle came from Cal as he wrapped his arms around me and said sweetly, "Oh, Jen . . . " He hugged me until I had gained composure. "Ari is fine," he whispered into my ear with confidence, "She's doing really well with your mom and loves her school. And she has me! I'm her dad," he said with a little laugh. "Ella needs you right now. They're both going to be fine. This is just how it has to be for a while," he soothed. "You don't think Ari will forget me or hurt because I was gone for so long?" I said, wiping tears from my eyes. "No, Jen. She probably won't even remember. I know she'll be glad to have you back, but she's doing really good," Cal reassured me.

How did I have such a wonderful and amazing husband? The knowledge that I could not do any of this without him by my side overwhelmed my spirit. Jesus had taken us both on our own individual journeys during the long and somewhat tumultuous wait for Ella's birth, only to unite us and make our bond unbreakable through supernatural means. The realization of God's goodness soaked into my soul, and with it came a deep-rooted peace. I would never stop missing my precious daughter, Ariana, but for now, God had provided a perfect solution for each of my girls and was sustaining them just as He was doing for Cal and me.

"We were under great pressure, far beyond our ability to endure,
so that we despaired even of life. Indeed, in our hearts we felt
the sentence of death. But this happened that we might not rely
on ourselves but on God, who raises the dead. He has delivered
us from such a deadly peril, and he will deliver us. On him
we have set our hope that he will continue to deliver us."

ॐ 2 Corinthians 1:8b-10

. . . .

Sitting by Ella's hospital bed never got old to me. I just stared at her; minutes passed, but I could still find new features and intricate details that made up her precious little body. And if my eyes were ever peeled away from my new little babe, there was plenty to gawk at in the hospital room as well. Machines, monitors, and lights embellished the wall behind Ella's bed; the nurses even made a sweet little scrapbook page with Ella's footprints, birth date, and a photo of her that was posted on a board above her bed.

As I gazed around the room, I noticed Ella's nurse who was dedicated specifically to her 100 percent of the time, and was thankful for the continuous care she was receiving. Other rooms housed two or three babies who were all sharing one nurse. Our first day in the unit, I had asked the nurse caring for Ella, "Why does Ella have a nurse all to herself?" She responded, "Well . . . " I could see that she was choosing her words carefully. "Ella is a very sick baby. Other babies are in here sometimes for a little extra oxygen, or other times they just need their heart rates or oxygen levels monitored, but Ella is a high-risk baby. There's so much going on with her little body that things change by the second. I need to be with her all the time so I can notice any change in her coloring, any dips in blood pressure or drops in her heart rate. They'll keep Ella closely monitored until she's well enough to share a nurse with another patient," she concluded.

As Ella's neonatologist, Dr. Render, came into the room to check on her, my mind snapped back to the moment at hand. He stepped closer to Ella's bed and gave me a warm smile and then allowed his gaze to fall on my sedated daughter. He seemed to be looking her up and down, assessing each miniature part of her body. After flipping through several pages on his clipboard and comparing them by looking over the nurse's shoulder at the notes she was taking, he took a deep breath and returned his focus to me. "How are you doing?" he asked sincerely. "Good. We're doing really well," I answered peacefully. "I've got a couple pieces of information for you," he said thoughtfully, trying to put what he had to say into simple words. "Ella did have a brain bleed at birth, and after the neurologist reviewed the X-rays, it's been determined that it was a grade one bleed." Without allowing Dr. Render to finish, I interrupted, "What is a grade one bleed?"

"A grade one bleed is the smallest bleed there is. It's definitely not a brain bleed we'll need to operate on. We're going to keep our eye on it to make sure that it dissolves, but normally it's not a huge problem. She does have a slight chance of developing cerebral palsy because of it, but again, the chances are slim. So that's the good news." I liked how Dr. Render spoke. Very upbeat and encouraging, often breaking between sentences to smile at me, but the look he gave me next was a bit confusing. He looked down at his clipboard and a look of profound thought and disappointment covered his face as his eyebrows pinched together and created deep creases between his eyes.

"We've taken some X-rays of Ella's abdomen because she's been unable to urinate. The X-rays showed that her urine is backing up into her kidneys, which are covered in cysts." He paused then, and breathing a little harder, continued, "She may not make it. With these cysts and her body's inability to properly function—mainly her lungs, dangerously low blood pressure, and dysfunctional kidneys that are close to failing—her chances are just not good. We're going to do an ultrasound to verify." His eyes, full of compassion, looked directly into mine before he gazed down at the floor with a look of failure. "I'm so sorry," he finished. At his words, I felt like melting into another puddle of tears, but wanted to stay strong in front of the nurses and in front of Ella. She was sedated, but it was my belief that she could feel what was going on in the room. If I was tense, I thought that she'd be able to feel it.

So, as soon as it was time for me to pump again, I excused myself to go to my hospital room. When I arrived in my room, I exhaled and allowed myself to really breathe. Tears stung my cheeks as I revisited what the doctor had just told me. *She may not make it. I'm so sorry.* Would a doctor say that if it wasn't serious? No! He'd only say it if he thought it was true or very likely to happen. In a rush of emotion, I felt completely powerless. When would this war for Ella's life be over? Would I ever rest in the fact that she was OK?

In a moment of complete surrender, I knelt helplessly on the cold hospital room floor in my tear-stained hospital gown and began to pray. I ardently prayed for my girl, but as hard as I tried, my mind and heart kept being led to praise. Words of thanks poured from my mouth, exalting the Most High God for the things he *had* done and was *doing* in Ella's life. The prayer continued and continued until my knees were stuck flat to the tiles, and when I was done, a spirit of complete peace washed over me. I had handed the life of my baby over to the King of Kings and Lord of Lords yet again. And just as the Scripture promises in Philippians 4:6-7, I received God's perfect peace: "Do not be anxious about anything, but in everything, by prayer and petition, with thanksgiving, present your requests to God. And the peace of God, which transcends all understanding, will guard your hearts and your minds in Christ Jesus" (Philippians 4:6-7).

....

I woke up on the third day after Ella's birth to Dr. Render entering my hospital room. He was panting and out of breath, almost like he had run all the way from the NICU just to tell me some important tidbit of information—*or* maybe like he was nervous and about to relay some really bad news. Immediately I was ready to listen to what he had to say.

"I just had to tell you right away," he began, "the ultrasound results are back, and what we thought were cysts on Ella's kidneys are actually pockets of fluid. We inserted a catheter to Ella's bladder, and as soon as we did that, the kidneys released the fluid and it came right out," he said, almost jumping for joy. "The bad news is that her urine is not coming through the catheter, it's sort of spilling out all around it, but I presume this is a problem that we can work with," he said with a smile.

My mind was trying to process the information that had just been heaped onto my groggy brain. "So, Ella's going to be OK?" I asked in a sleepy daze. "Well, she's not out of the woods," he said. We'd heard that phrase countless times since Ella's birth, as doctors tried their best not to get our hopes up about getting to keep our new little blessing. "But her kidneys will not be the problem if something does go wrong," he continued encouragingly. "Thank you so much!" I squeaked as I blinked away tears with my half-open eyes. We had just witnessed another miracle!

When he left the room, a trance-like joy settled over me. "Thank you, God," I breathed. What a quick answer to a heart-felt prayer. "Who is like our God?" my mind kept saying over and over again. I had so many reasons to praise God today. My baby was alive and life was good.

13

Juggling Life

AT FIRST, CAL AND I had decided that it would be best to keep Ariana away from the NICU, for many reasons—the biggest being that we were concerned that she wouldn't be able to handle the strange sight of her baby sister connected to all sorts of tubes and machines. We feared that her little one-and-a-half-year-old mind wouldn't be able to process what was going on and would cause her anxiety or worry, but after the seeming eternity of the three long days of Ella's life, Cal and I had both changed our minds. Ariana knew that our baby had been born and people were constantly asking her about her baby sister. Because of that, combined with the fact that we didn't know how long we'd have Ella, we decided it was time to introduce our girls to each other.

By this point, Ariana was used to hospital trips to visit her mommy, but this one was different. She had already learned exactly how to get to my hospital room, but now, she had to learn a different branch of the hospital. One of her favorite features upon her first visit to the NICU was the telephone that hung just outside the locked doors of the unit. Immediately, she decided that she would be the one to call in to the desk. When the magical doors flung open, they exposed a waiting room filled with magazines, snack bar, bathrooms, and a wondrous play area with books, crayons, toys of all types, and a great fish tank filled with several colorful specimens. That first day, we didn't want to take time to play, so we did our best to block Ari's view of the incredible play area and ushered her through the second set of locked doors that led into the NICU itself.

Our first stop, of course, was the scrub room. Ari had a blast making bubbles and using the special brush and sponge that were required for scrubbing in. Having her in the NICU made Cal and I very self-conscious because she was making a *lot* more noise than was usual and because she traveled at one speed: fast. She didn't *walk* anywhere. Because Ariana was almost two years old, she was becoming very *busy*! It was quite a challenge to keep those increasingly independent and active hands away from all the lurking germs and dirt that seemed to specifically allure them.

We finally made it to Ella's bedside, and what happened next is so special. Wrapped in her daddy's big arms, Ari peered down at her tiny sister. For a moment, Ari just looked. Then she peered over at me and questioned, "Baby?" I smiled warmly and answered, "Yes! That's our baby!" She looked at Ella again and then at my stomach. Pointing to my abdomen, Ari asked, "Baby . . . tummy?" I took that to mean that she was wondering if the baby on the bed was the one that had been in my tummy, so I told her, "Yes, that's the baby that was in Mommy's tummy. Now Mommy's tummy is empty!" As if a light bulb had gone off in her head she looked back at her sister and adamantly pointed her index finger at her and said, "El-la," emphasizing the "L" sound by sticking her tongue way out of her mouth. "Yes, sweetie, that's Ella!"

For another moment, her curious eyes scanned the lifeless body, and for a second I thought maybe the sight was too much for her, but when Ariana spoke, my thoughts were proved incorrect. She gazed back up at me and simply asked, "Up?" "Aha!" I thought. "She's just trying to figure out how to play with her new baby sister because she wants Ella to get 'up.'" At that point, Calvin chimed in, "No, kiddo, she's sick, so she has to lay there and let the doctors fix her, but she's our baby—we'll get to take her home in a long, long time when she's all better."

After Ari seemed to have everything all figured out, she just kept saying "baby" and "El-la," with her tongue hanging out of her mouth each time she said it. Calvin helped Ari examine her baby sister for the next several moments, identifying Ella's belly button, legs, arms, and tummy, until Ari decided that she wanted to give Ella a "high five." Realizing that it could be dangerous for a baby who has sensory sensitivity to come into contact with the rougher-than-usual touch (to put it lightly) of a one-and-a-half-year-old, we came up with the "baby high five."

"Ari, can you point your finger out like this?" I asked her as I stretched my index finger forward and curled the rest of my fingers into my palm. She positioned her finger into a point and proudly held it up so I could see. After acknowledging Ari's ability to point, I took my finger and placed it gently into Ella's limp palm and said, "Look Ari, this is a baby high five! Do you want to try?" Calvin lowered Ari to Ella's level and surprisingly, Ari was gentle. She placed her finger into Ella's palm exactly how I had shown her, "Baby high fi," Ari said with a smile. It was precious. Having our two girls together was wonderful. The sense of completeness I felt was enough to fill my heart a hundred times over.

Soon after the high five, Ari's attention span had been maxed out and the button-pushing temptation became too great, so Ari's trip to the NICU came to a close. We took her out and she waved, "Bye-bye, baby El-la." As Cal and I walked our oldest daughter out of the NICU, we exchanged a glance that said it all. When I looked into Cal's calm eyes, I could see relief and realized that our worries had been unwarranted. Ariana had been able to see her young sister, and even though she didn't understand in adult terms what was going on with her, she knew that Ella was sick and needed the doctors. It was simple to her little mind. She knew that Ella would see the doctors, get better, and then come home to be her sister. As Ariana frolicked worriless out of the hospital doors, my heart wished it could feel the freedom that my young child felt, even after seeing an unusual and even scary sight.

Then I realized—Jesus told us we could have that same freedom! My mind reflected upon the verse I mentioned earlier, how through prayer, God will give us the peace that transcends all understanding. He is so faithful to give without ceasing, if only we ask Him. And oh, that we'd have faith like a child! In the Bible, Jesus explains to his disciples who is the greatest in the kingdom of heaven, "I tell you the truth, unless you change and become like little children, you will never enter the kingdom of heaven. Therefore, whoever humbles himself like this child is the greatest in the kingdom of heaven" (Matthew 18:3-4).

And in Isaiah 11:6, it says, "A little child will lead them." How true! Our little Ari had seen the grave situation, asked her questions, and then moved on to enjoy the beautiful world that her God had given her. Jesus says in the book of Matthew, "Who of you by worrying can add a single hour to his life?" (Matthew 6:27). And, in 1 Thessalonians 5:16 (NCV), we are commanded to, "Always be joyful. Pray continually, and give thanks whatever happens." If God really does have everything in His hands and doesn't want us to worry, but commands us to be joyful always, I should be able to rest in His peace, no matter what.

In many ways, our little Ariana did lead us, and oh, how thankful we are for that. The God of all creation carries us, and everything is done for His glory and in His ultimate love for us, even if our blinders are so large that we can't see one inch in front of our noses!"Lord, give me faith like a child!" was my prayer in that moment.

....

For a week, Ella remained sedated. She was on more medication than seemed healthy: first, the sedation medication, then morphine (for all the pain her little body was experiencing), blood pressure meds, a drug to help enlarge her veins and allow more blood and oxygen to filter through her body, and antibiotics. Then there were the countless wires, tubes and machines pumping and calculating to keep her body ticking. The thing I kept my eye on closest was Ella's ventilator. The tube stretched all the way down her throat, bringing oxygen directly to her underdeveloped lungs.

Up to this point, they had been blowing 100 percent oxygen into her small body. With the ventilator running at maximum just to keep her little life sustained, the risk is that when there are high oxygen levels mixed with long periods of time, it can wreak havoc on undeveloped eyes. So, for every day and every hour that Ella was receiving such high levels of oxygen, they feared that her eyes were being damaged more and more. But there was no way to tell until an actual eye exam was performed, which would not occur until several weeks later. All we could do until then was hope and pray and be absolutely content with the second of life that we were being blessed with in that instant.

In that first week, Calvin and I tried to figure out how to juggle responsibilities with parenthood and life in general. After I was discharged from the hospital, I was able to stay in a room at the local Ronald McDonald house just two blocks from Ella's hospital, which was 30 minutes from home. Calvin and Ari remained at my parent's house for the convenience of having my parents around when he left at midnight for work. I even fell into a routine as I cared daily for Ella; 6:00 a.m. started my day when the alarm blared at me to pump more breast milk (which Ella was still unable to take, even in her feed tube, because her stomach was too young and fragile to handle any substance). After showering and preparing for the day, I went straight to Ella's side at the hospital where I stayed and talked to her, read to her, and other times just sat with her, only breaking to pump every three hours. Then, at noon, I returned to the McDonald house to eat some lunch and put my legs up.

Because of my C-section and long hours with my legs in a seated position at the hospital, I was having terrible swelling and was ordered to keep my legs up for at least a couple hours each day. Some people say that when you have large ankles that blend in with your calves, they're called "cankles." Well, with the swelling from my larger-than-normal C-section, I joked that because my whole leg kind of stayed the same size all the way from my thigh to my ankles, I had "thighnkles." When I was finally finished with my "leg up time," I would return to the hospital, sometimes skipping dinner to stay with Ella until late into the night, even until midnight, just so that I could soak up every second I could with my precious baby girl.

Whenever a family member would come to visit Ella and me, I'd have to coordinate with them what time would work for my schedule between pumping and Ella's "cares" (when the baby is changed, cleaned, and repositioned every three hours), and meet them in the lobby of the NICU since security was so tight. Hospital life was starting to become a way of life.

Each night once I arrived back at the Ronald McDonald house, I'd slide into bed and just get my eyes closed before I was awoken by the annoying sound of my alarm clock, which went off every three hours so that I could pump. Waking up at night to nurse a hungry baby is hard enough; waking up to the irritating noise of an alarm clock is even worse. With a baby, you can sit in low-lit room snuggled up in a cozy rocking chair or even lay in bed and doze while the baby is nursing in the comfort of your own home, but when I pumped in the Ronald Mc Donald House, I was forced to flip on the light so that I could attach and ready all the pieces of the pump and sit upright for 20 long minutes while I pumped. After that, I was not free to lay back down and sleep. No! I had to package and label my milk, slip down to the basement, and place the newly pumped life-giving liquid into my space in the freezer designated for the storage of breast milk.

After returning to my room, I'd wash out the pumping bottles and get everything ready for the next session that, by that time, would only be about two and a half hours away. This is why most of the moms I met in the NICU went to formula; pumping was just too much, not to mention the time it took away from their new baby during the day, often causing them to miss "cares," the highlights of the day. I often thought, especially in the middle of the night, about going to formula once Ella started handling "feeds" through the tube that led to her premature stomach, but as quickly as the thought came, I dismissed it. Something in me was just repulsed by my selfish desire to give up.

I know now that I was experiencing conflicting emotions that most moms of preemies go through. There are incredible amounts of guilt for silly things that seem gigantically huge in the moment. Thoughts or actions that cause tremendous amounts of guilt could be anything from giving up on pumping, or like me, even considering giving up. There is guilt anytime the mother leaves the baby; nothing seems excusable in the mother's mind. It doesn't matter if you need to use the restroom, eat lunch, take a shower, go home to care for others; no matter what the case may be, any time that is spent away from your new little baby has guilt attached to it.

I am not sure what other moms go through or the intensity of what they feel while their children are in the NICU, but for me, my emotions were extreme. It may have been linked to Ella's critical status, that at any moment she could die; but whatever it was, if I had to be away from her for any amount of time it was as if my heart was being brutally shredded to pieces. It was especially bad if my family had planned something special or fun, (1) because I had to travel to our home city, Nampa, to get to the event, which put at least 30 minutes between Ella and me, and (2) because if I was having fun, something inside me felt like up-chucking and spewing my guilt, fear, and hurt all over everyone, because if Ella was plugged to machines, wires, and tubes, just to stay alive, how could I be out, away from her, enjoying myself? Guilt. It was Satan's biggest weapon in my life, and if you're reading this and have a baby in the NICU or a child who spends long periods of time in the hospital, he is hoping to use this on you as well.

This is when God emphasized to me the importance of clothing myself in the Armor of God each and every day, and sometimes, every second.

"Finally, be strong in the Lord and in his mighty power. Put on the full armor of God so that you can take your stand against the devil's schemes. For our struggle is not against flesh and blood, but against the rulers, against the authorities, against the powers of this dark world and against the spiritual forces of evil in the heavenly realms. Therefore put on the full armor of God, so that when the day of evil comes, you may be able to stand your ground, and after you have done everything, to stand. Stand firm then, with the belt of truth buckled around your waist, with the breastplate of righteousness in place, and with your feet fitted with the readiness that comes from the gospel of peace. In addition to all this, take up the shield of faith, with which you can extinguish all the flaming arrows of the evil one. Take the helmet of salvation and the sword of the Spirit, which is the word of God. And pray in the Spirit on all occasions with all kinds of prayers and requests. With this in mind, be alert and always keep on praying for all the saints."

෩ Ephesians 6:10-18

14

I Am with You

THE SOUNDS OF BEEPS AND dinging alarms signaling the end of a dose, a kinked line, a dipping heart rate, or plummeting oxygen levels all started to become a natural part of my surroundings. Even the daily way of life within the unit started to become somewhat normal. There was a certain code of conduct in the NICU that was only known by people who either worked there or frequented it. "Newbies" were obvious, oftentimes looking lost, speaking in a "loud" voice (anything above a whisper), or touching something "contaminated" from the "outside world" such as a purse, camera, or phone—or worse, blowing their noses without washing their hands.

The mood within the NICU was one all its own, a quiet and somber atmosphere. Nurses' faces sometimes gave sympathetic smiles, but mostly were stricken with the seriousness of their work. Scents of hand soap and sanitizer filled each room. It was a place where much was observed, but only spoken if it was deemed important. Each preemie was given the maximum opportunity to grow and sleep in long, uninterrupted spurts, so as to simulate the mother's womb as much as possible.

But even with the normality that was setting in, my heart still raced and adrenaline pulsed through my body every time Ella's alarm would warn that her oxygen was dipping or that her heart rate was dropping. The fact that she had a nurse stationed right with her was such a comfort, but I couldn't help but worry a bit about what would happen when and if Ella became well enough that she could share a nurse. What if the nurse was preoccupied with another baby when the dip came? What if I wasn't there to notify the nurse? What if? What if? What if? All the "what ifs" were completely overwhelming. In times like that, I would feel the complete peace of Jesus Christ come over my entire being and calm me from the inside out. He had this!

I remember the doctors told me that Ella had reached the maximum number of days that she could have lines running into her belly button and that she'd need another form of access into her frail little body. Ella had been receiving nutrients and medications and had given blood from this catheter that was threaded directly into her central artery system, but the risk of infection was becoming too great, so the doctors decided it was time to take out the lines that ran into her miniscule belly button and insert a PICC line (peripherally inserted central catheter) in her left arm to take over the distribution of nutrients, medication, or anything they needed to get into her system quickly. The line ran from the crease in Ella's elbow up around her shoulder and sat next to her heart, distributing its contents directly into her bloodstream. The PICC line was especially important to me because it was her source of "food." In her first week of life, Ella did not receive any breast milk or formula because her body could not yet handle it; only the nutrients that were imperative for survival were given into her bloodstream.

....

Soon after the PICC line was inserted into Ella's arm, her health started to regress at quite a rapid pace and many of her illnesses returned and progressively got worse. Ella's skin was sunken and gray; the life seemed to go out of her in just one day. It was absolutely terrifying to see our daughter go from a nice, pink color to the familiar death-like color she had in the first days of life. I wasn't ready to lose her.

After several X-rays, exams, and tests, they found that Ella's body was not making enough red blood cells. The solution to the problem was a full-body blood transfusion. I never really understood how blood transfusions worked until I actually saw the blood pumping into my tiny daughter. Since Ella already had the PICC line in, they were able to use that point of access to introduce the new blood. I was surprised at the many hours it took for the blood to be transmitted into her tiny body. Six hours passed before the transfusion was complete. The difference in Ella's appearance after the procedure was absolutely amazing. Ella's coloring was fresh and new, pink and healthy. It turned out that the PICC line was an incredibly *good* thing and had been inserted just in time to transmit the new blood! I felt as if we'd cheated death yet again.

....

As I rounded the corner into Ella's hospital room on her eighth day of life, I noticed several people around her bed, which sent a tingle of absolute fear up my spine. The hair on the back of my neck stood on end as I approached the people I recognized to be respiratory therapists and nurses who huddled around my baby. As the never-ending fear that Ella had died crept up and clouded any sense of clarity I had previously had, I did my best to push it down and remain calm until I could figure out what had happened. Every day since Ella was born, we fought the odds. When she was born "dead" and then resuscitated to life, it was as if we'd stolen a secret gift and were soon due to give it back. Constantly, doctors reminded us of Ella's near-death state and how unlikely it would be for her to live. Even their words were harsher reminders than were needed, for anyone could see as they looked upon that tiny frame of a person that death was crowding in.

Her body was tiny and yet, completely enormous pumped full of medications to maintain function because she couldn't do it herself. Her little frame was so underdeveloped that she didn't even have eyelashes and looked as if her eyes were completely sealed shut. I had never seen my baby take a breath of her own or even make a tiny peep. Never had I thought I'd long for the cry of a baby as much as I did at this point (especially after having a baby like Ariana who was up each night every one-and-a-half to two hours)! I didn't even know what color Ella's eyes were or what she looked like without tubes in her face. I had not yet experienced holding her or feeling her breath on my neck as I burped her. No, the truth was brutally evident, constantly pushing to the foreground, trying to make itself known—our baby displayed the look of death. And just as the doctors had told us for the last week, any day could be her last.

I felt as if the panic within me was boiling to such a point that it would just erupt out of me in a scream. All these thoughts had bombarded me as soon as I'd rounded the corner of Ella's hospital room, and now, as I stood, momentarily waiting, almost ready to have an emotional break-down, God spoke to my heart, "*I Am with you.*" The words blew into my heart and brought a strength and tranquility I had known throughout this journey. In fact, it was the very strength that had been given to me the night my water broke as I waited in my closet for a phone call from my doctor. Jesus was with *me*! The creator of the universe lived in *me*! He'd already given me a miracle with the life of my child; why was I counting on devastation when He had promised me life?

With my new sense of composure and utter serenity, I entered a situation that I did not know the outcome to.

....

I had never seen such beautiful eyes. With the exception of the birth of my daughter, Ariana, this was the most precious moment of my life. Eleven days old now, Ella was finally "allowed" to wake up. Two days earlier many of Ella's life-threatening ailments had lifted! She had faced such critical disorders as unstable blood pressure (that had been maintained by three different medications), inability to urinate and possible kidney failure, inability to have a stool, *and* failure to breathe without a ventilator, but now, so much had changed. The day I had come in to find nurses and therapists working diligently around her was the day that she had been taken off of the "jet" (a rapid ventilator that pushes tiny puffs of air into the lungs) and placed onto the conventional vent. The group huddle had been a *good* thing. The move from the "jet" to the conventional ventilator was a sign of improvement!

And as each of these medical hurdles were being jumped, the only explanation the doctor could give us was, "Well, I don't know what to say. She should not be doing this well. Just don't get your hopes up. She's not out of the woods." It was as if he was nervous we'd take Ella's signs of improvement as a passing grade and assume that she would be moving up to a new class when really, in his mind, she had somehow gotten the correct score on the test without studying. To the doctor, Ella's new forward movement didn't add up, and because he could not see a medical explanation as to why she was doing so well, he assumed it would not last long.

Shortly after the doctor had given his report on the positive changes in Ella's body, Ella's nurse felt the need to reiterate the unusual status of Ella's life: "This is really odd. These babies never do this well. Just don't get your hopes up; many times these babies will take three steps forward and two steps back." It was apparent to us that the amazing advances that Ella was experiencing were not normal and the medical staff wasn't quite sure what to do, except to warn us against any excitement about improvement. Her little body had had so many insurmountable obstacles, it was highly unlikely that they could really all just go away.

But we knew exactly what was happening. God was at work. And now, after Ella had been on the conventional ventilator for two days and was beginning to wake up, I just stared and inspected every inch of my beautiful daughter. Occasionally, her leg would twitch or she'd open her eyes. Her movement was a glorious sign of life, one that I had longed to see for almost two weeks! Ella still had all of the same tubes and wires on her small body, but the fact that she was waking up and starting to look *alive* was more than we could have hoped for!

After having the absolute privilege of examining my alive and awake little baby and feeling the sense that I'd received a new gift, a sensation of absolute gratitude and awe flooded my being and I knew that I had to get out of the NICU before I broke down in front of everyone. I quickly made my way to the Ronald McDonald house, into my room and onto my bed, notebook in hand as words and tears of thanksgiving and amazement poured onto the lines of paper. This is the poem I wrote that day:

My NICU Baby: ELLA BREANNE

Lying motionless on a hospital bed, My little baby rests her head. Her body, so tiny and oh, so frail. Stuck in her lifeless jail. Cords, wires, tubes and machines, I know not what it all means. Alarms and bells are blaring, And I just stand there staring.

What can I do to help my child, While my heart is racing wild? I feel so powerless, so out of control, My chest caves in like an empty hole.

About to surrender to panic and fear, But what's this that's drawing near?
My God! My God! It's YOU, I know! That's saving me from the final blow.

You swooped up my baby in your mammoth arms, And
suddenly I don't hear the alarms. Peace, quiet, calm fill
my heart. You always cared, right from the start.

Your love is amazing, it knows no bounds. It fills me so
full, my heart loudly pounds. What's this? My child awakes!
She looks and stretches. Her first breath she takes!

Before, my baby was so lifeless. How can this be? Just that it IS! I
can clearly see. God worked a miracle, Her name is Ella Bre.

By: Jennifer Wilkins

15

Signs of Life

"WOULD YOU LIKE TO HOLD HER?" the nurse asked me when I returned to the hospital. My mind froze. It was as if the words went into my head, but then just stopped, occupying space, until my brain could begin to process what I had just been asked. Would I *like* to hold her? What kind of a question is that? Of course I would like to hold her! My heart began to race with excitement at the idea of being that close to my precious child. "Yes!" I responded eagerly. "Will it be kangaroo care?" I had heard from other moms in the NICU that the style in which they were required to hold their premature babies was called "kangaroo care."

When mothers held their babies kangaroo style, the babies were placed on the mother's bare chest while the baby sported only a diaper, so that their skin made complete contact with the mother's. I had been told that a mother's body will monitor the temperature of the baby and actually heat up or cool down, depending on what the baby needs. Just another amazing example of how intricately and wonderfully God made our bodies!

"Yes, babies as little as yours need to be held skin to skin. If you can wait a few minutes, I'll get a respiratory therapist in here to help get us situated," she told me. "A respiratory therapist? Is it going to stress Ella's airways or compromise her in any way for me to hold her? I do want to be close to her, but is it good for her?" I wondered. After voicing my concern, the nurse assured me that it was very beneficial for babies to be near to their mothers and that it wasn't a problem at all to get us set up, but after my fears were eased, a new idea crept in.

"Shouldn't Cal be the first to hold her? I have been the one who gets to be with Ella everyday and see each of her milestones firsthand." As my mind continued to sort things out I knew that today should be Cal's day. In a few minutes he would be at the hospital because it was his short day at work; tomorrow however, was a long day, which made his visits with Ella much shorter. And the one rule about kangaroo care is that you have to hold for at least an hour.

One reason for requiring parents to hold their babies for at least one hour is that it takes so long to get the baby situated with all the tubes and wires, and if you're going to hold the baby for just a few minutes, it doesn't make much sense. Another reason is that they want babies to get as much sleep as possible between periods of being awake, because sleep time is grow time. Most of these babies should still be in the womb, so they don't want to be moving them around needlessly. Yes, today would be the day for Calvin to hold Ella because I wasn't sure when the next chance would come for him to have at least an hour. I'd take my turn tomorrow.

Preparing Ella and Calvin for his "hold" was one of the most nerve-racking experiences of my life. Because of the way the tubes and wires were strung through the slots in the bed, the nurses and therapists were going to have to detach Ella from her ventilator and IVs during her transfer from the bed to Cal's arms. The plan was to reattach everything once he had her safely in his arms.

There were three medical personnel working just with Ella while Cal took off his shirt and put on an open-fronted hospital gown. Then, when the respiratory therapist had Ella ready to unhook from the ventilator, the nurse gave Cal instructions on how to carefully lift Ella's miniature body from the bed, place her on his chest, and sit slowly in the recliner positioned behind him.

It sounded easy enough, but the actual event was a bit more complicated. First, the cords and wires were gathered by the assistant, and once those were collected and out of the way, the respiratory therapist unhooked the tube from Ella's mouth, leaving one end of the ventilation hose down her throat and the other end sticking out of her mouth waiting to be reattached to the tube that supplied the life-saving oxygen. Once the oxygen was disconnected, things happened quickly.

I was so impressed with Cal. He was so calm, just leaning down and gently scooping up Ella's little body and slowly leaning her forward to rest on his chest. This is the part that made me go nutty, because while Ella was detached from her oxygen, the levels in her blood dropped quickly and caused her alarms to go off like crazy. Not only was she desaturating, but her heart rate was dropping quickly, and it seemed that every bell that could go off, was going off. I found myself wondering if holding her was worth almost losing her. I felt adrenaline kicking in, and it was all I could do to just stand back and watch as my body was ablaze with readiness and nearing the phase of panic. I really felt that she might die in that moment as she was disconnected from the life support.

The health professionals all kept their cool and worked diligently to reconnect Ella's ventilator and adjust her medication to stabilize the situation. Though I'm sure the medical staff would have never allowed this move if they hadn't thought it safe, it sure gave me the scare of a lifetime. Through the entire ordeal, Calvin stood there, with his tiny daughter situated on his warm chest, calm and as happy as could be. He had been waiting for this moment since Ella had been born and was enjoying every second of it. Once Ella had stabilized and the situation was under control, Calvin carefully stepped backward to the waiting recliner and slowly lowered himself into the chair. After he was seated, the medical staff once again crowded in, and in turn, listened to Ella's heart and breathing, repositioned her limbs, added blankets, and taped tubes and wires onto the chair so that none of them would kink.

After everything was all settled, I gazed down at my husband and daughter and was witness to the most beautiful sight. The love of my life and father of my children, with eyes fixed on the tiny bundle that lay on his body, had a look of complete satisfaction and love radiating from his face as he gazed at his premature daughter. It's a memory that's locked up and treasured in my heart forever and ever. I will never forget how peaceful Calvin looked, or the glow of joy that absolutely shone from his face after relaxing in the chair with his precious baby whom he had waited so long to hold—*or* the heart-pounding craziness that brought us to that moment.

Later, when I asked Calvin about the intense moments leading up to his "hold," he told me that he was completely at ease and didn't have a worry at all. "Well, Jen, they wouldn't have done it if they didn't think it was safe for Ella," he had later informed me with a confident grin.

....

Day eleven of Ella's life continued to be a day of blessing. Not only did Calvin get to hold Ella for the first time, but it was also the day that they gave Ella her first little "meal" of breast milk (colostrum) through the feed tube that ran into her nose, down her throat, and into her tummy. It was only a few cubic centimeters, or cc (30 cc is an ounce) for the first feed, but it was exciting. She spit it all up, but still, it was a step in the right direction.

A few hours later, they tried to feed her again, and this time, she kept half of it down. The way they determined how well her body was digesting the feed was by putting a syringe on the end of her feed tube and pulling up whatever fluid was in her stomach three hours after the feed. After measuring the amount of substance that had been extracted, they reintroduce it to her stomach by pushing it back through the syringe little by little. The first time I saw the extraction and reentry of the half-digested breast milk, I was thoroughly grossed out, but after watching them do it after every feed, it became a normal part of my day. At times, I even got to "feed" Ella when the timing pump was unavailable by putting the breast milk in the feed tube and holding it above Ella's head while the liquid slowly made its way down the tube and into her tummy. This was just one of many unusual things that became ordinary to us during this time.

Another routine that was becoming somewhat natural was changing Ella's diaper. At first, when Ella had only been a few days old, I had been incredibly uncomfortable trying to do the nerve-racking task. She had only weighed three pounds, and at one point, after she had urinated out all of the medication, had weighed something like two pounds, 10 ounces. So, as you can imagine, I felt like I was going to break her every time I lifted up her tiny little legs; it was as if they were toothpicks that would snap at any moment. The first time I changed her diaper, I had a little surprise awaiting me. No, not the "surprise" you're thinking. There was no poop—I wish that had been it, for the sight would have been much more normal to my eyes and would have meant that her body was actually functioning properly. As I lifted her little legs for the first time to wipe her little rear, I was shocked to see yet another sign that our baby had been born way too early: she had no "cheeks." There was no crack, no fat of any kind, just a flat back that never ended. Now, however, after beginning her breast milk feeds, she was starting to gain weight and was beginning to look a bit more "normal."

....

The next day was my turn to hold Ella. As we went through the whole ordeal of unhooking and reconnecting all the machines, I realized how it had all been worth it the day before to Cal. As I looked down at my precious child and enjoyed the feel of her warm body on my chest, I was reminded of what a precious gift God had given to me. Ella's nurse that day, Jo, put a tiny bow on Ella's head and snapped a few pictures of me holding her. While I reclined and cherished my little piece of heaven, my mind was taken to a place I had been not many weeks earlier, in my hospital room. I had been waiting and wondering what God's plan was and how it would unfold. I had known that God was going to bless us with our little Ella, but had no idea how He was going to make it all happen. Then, as my mind raced back to the present, I was amazed at the way He had worked. No, Ella was not born perfectly, and no, she was still not "out of the woods" yet, but she was here, and I was enjoying every moment that God blessed us with.

This was the first time I held her (before the nurse applied the bow on Ella's head).

Really, if we would have had the chance to change everything, or to rewind time, or even to wish away the pregnancy itself, we would not have changed a second. Only our sometimes poor attitudes would we have transformed for the better, if given the opportunity. With each trial, God overcame, and with each devastating blow, God brought others closer to Himself. Even in the moment we were currently in, with Ella on life support, me living away from Calvin and Ariana, and with life sort of on pause, God was working.

I had typed and printed out the poem that I had written about Ella and hung it on the wall of her hospital room. Many times I would come in to find one of her nurses, aides, or therapists reading it. When they'd become aware that I was there, they'd turn with misty eyes, give me a faint smile, and move on to do some more work. The longer we were in the NICU, the more medical staff would come up to us and share their feelings about Ella or declare their thoughts on our family. I remember one nurse breezed into Ella's room one day and noticed me sitting by Ella's bedside and said, "I just wish we could send all our babies home with you guys," her eyes searching mine like she was looking for some hidden secret, seeming to try and pull back layers to find out how we could be so dedicated and always cheerful. She continued, "Most of our babies don't come from very good homes." Her eyes conveyed a look of concern, and worry creased her brows as I could tell this was an issue she struggled with every day.

Another time, our favorite nurse, Lailani, a fellow-believer in Christ, shared with us that the NICU was buzzing about our family. Many had mentioned that there was something different about our family, and nurses often vied for who would get to care for Ella. It was an amazing time of miracles in our lives and the lives of those around us. No, if given the chance, we would not change a thing. God was working and we were so blessed to be a part of it.

16

Milestones

MY EYES SEARCHED THE PILE, looking for a stamp that would appropriately represent the month of July. "There, a sun wearing sunglasses, that ought to do it," I thought as I picked it up, pressed it down on the yellowish-orange ink pad, and transferred the color onto the calendar I was decorating. All of us were making calendars that would mark our children's milestones once they were discharged from the NICU. Once a week, the NICU hosted a mom's craft time to bring us together and create a safe place to share and vent. This time, I happened to be there with my friend, Jan, whom I'd met in the NICU because we'd both spent significant time there caring for our babies.

It was only the first week in June, Ella was almost a month old, and she still had almost two months to go to reach her due date of July 17. Looking at the calendar made me excited as I realized all the milestones that I'd already be able to post for the month of May. It had been slow going, but Ella had made giant leaps in the right direction.

Only two weeks after she was born, Ella had been taken off the ventilator and put onto CPAP (continuous positive airway pressure). CPAP delivered forced air through a device that attached to Ella's head and held two enormous prongs in Ella's nose, instead of through a tube traveling down her throat. Normally, CPAP masks are a little plastic dome placed over a child's nose, but Ella got the old-fashioned kind that delivered the oxygen through prongs. CPAP was supposed to be less invasive, but to a mother's eyes, it looked three times more invasive than the ventilator. The prongs that were inserted into Ella's nostrils were connected to two large plastic tubes that framed Ella's face and were held by a rubber band strapped around the individual tubes and fastened to safety pins on Ella's hospital cap. The machine forced oxygen down into Ella's lungs and kept her airways open with the constant pressure. This new form of breathing was unsightly, but it had been a step forward.

This is Ella wearing CPAP.

Along with Ella's move off of the vent came a physical move. Since birth, Ella had been lying on a little table-like bed, wearing only a diaper so that she'd be easily available to the doctors and nurses as she required daily blood draws, exams, and other procedures. Because she was no longer on life support, the nurses no longer needed her in such an "accessible" place, so she was able to be placed in a protective bed called an incubator that was fitted with a plastic cover to keep Ella completely enclosed and away from any outside germs. The only way to access our girl was to pull open the lid that was secured by several little latches, or to open the little plastic doors that were made in order to provide entry for hands without exposing Ella to the germy air. When Ella was moved from her open bed to this incubator, she was placed in clothing. It didn't matter how tiny the outfit, she still swam in it. Newborn clothes were an impossibility, and even preemie clothes had to be rolled up several times over just to function as clothing.

With Ella's continued improvements, she was no longer the only patient assigned to a nurse. Ella now had to share a nurse with two other babies. Even with the forward motion of Ella's health, somehow we still had the sense that she was not out of the woods yet. It seemed that her body just kept coming up with more and more issues that needed to be ironed out. But with every ailment, there had been an answer, and doctors and nurses alike had one comment that we heard almost daily: "She should not be doing this well!" And every time we heard that phrase, we graciously smiled and said, "We know *who's* in charge of her little life; it's God, and He's hard at work."

Also, in Ella's first month, she continued to be fed my breast milk through her feed tube, but on occasion, I was allowed to try and nurse her. This created an intense incentive for me to keep on pumping. I knew that breast milk was very beneficial for "normal" babies and had been told how crucial it was for preemies to receive breast milk. So with that information and my desire to be able to nurse her, accompanied by the requirement that babies had to be able to eat on their own without a feed tube in order to be discharged, I was gung ho about getting her off the feed tube. It had been very slow going, and some days Ella wouldn't have enough energy to nurse at all. Every day was a roller coaster of emotion with big steps forward and then several steps back. But somehow, Ella had almost made it to the one month mark, and we were celebrating.

My attention was brought back to the NICU's craft room with the other moms chatting about their babies and families as they finished up their calendars. The weekly craft time proved to be incredibly refreshing. I enjoyed hearing other people's stories and being able to share the peace we were gifted with because of our faith in Jesus Christ. It was apparent to me why Ella had traveled such a rough course now, because if she hadn't, there'd be no way I could relate with the other moms in the NICU or even have a credible story of God's amazing provision in our lives. Many families were struggling with life-threatening ordeals and long stints in the hospital. How would we have ever been able to be an example of God's grace and love to them if we hadn't endured a similar hardship?

I do remember that on this day, one of the moms was really distraught. My friend Jan and I took up the project of encouraging this woman. After hearing the sorrow in her voice and seeing the exhaustion in her face, we both offered a lending ear and open hearts to her. I had been in the NICU for a month at this point and in the hospital myself on bed rest for a month and a half, and Jan was almost to the 3 month mark, so we both had deep compassion for this woman who was hurting so intensely because of her baby's predicament. I sympathetically asked how long the woman had been in the NICU, assuming it'd probably been much longer than my one month stay. Exasperated, she replied, *"Two days!"* The words flew out of her mouth like it was the most incredibly unbelievable news anyone had ever announced, but it was all I could do not to giggle.

Jan and I exchanged looks and did our best to be encouraging and supportive to the woman who was falling apart in front of us, but part of me just wanted to smack her and say, "Pull yourself together! I've been here for 30 days! And Jan's been here for *three* months! My child has been fighting death, and your kid was born full-term just needing a little bit of oxygen and observation! You're going home tomorrow and I'm facing at least another two months in here!" Really, it was a bit comedic, but my heart did go out to her. Just because our situations had been more devastating than her two-day stay doesn't mean it was any easier for her to cope. After all, I had known all along that my pregnancy was high-risk, and this poor mother had gone to the hospital with a healthy pregnancy, just expecting to deliver a perfect baby boy, only to find out he had to stay for an extra two days. I imagined it would be difficult.

....

Since Ella had been placed in the incubator, the doctors started to talk more and more about how well Ella was progressing and what milestones she needed to reach before she could be sent home. What an adjustment in conversation had occurred over the last month! It seemed that not too long ago, the topic of discussion had been how to keep Ella alive. And now we were being informed on what goals needed to be met before Ella could go home! The first and most obvious objective was that Ella needed to be able to eat without the assistance of a feeding tube. The second target that needed to be hit was that she needed to be able to maintain her own body temperature without a bed heater. Next, she had to be gaining weight each day, and lastly, she had to pass her car seat study. (A car seat is brought into the baby's NICU room and monitors are attached to the child while the child lies in the car seat for an hour or so. Monitors read what's going on in the baby's body and look for signs of trouble processing oxygen or keeping a steady heart rate while seated in the new position.) I knew we still had a ways to go, because Ella was nowhere near reaching any of those goals in the next several days, but the fact that we had the list of objectives was a move in the right direction.

....

"Can you take her temperature for me, please?" Carol, Ella's nurse, asked as she handed me the thermometer and looked back down to her notes. "Sure," I said, feeling somewhat confident in helping with the daily routines. After unlatching and opening the plastic doors on the incubator and slipping my hands inside, I snuck the thermometer through the neck hole of Ella's baggy pajamas and under her arm to get an accurate read of her temperature. "35.5 degrees Celsius," I read back to Carol as she charted Ella's current vitals. Since I was not very familiar with temperatures in Celsius yet, I wasn't sure what the concerned look on Carol's face meant.

Brows furrowed and lips puckered off to the side, Carol flipped through the pages of Ella's chart, "Hmm," was the only sound that escaped from her lips as she rummaged through the sheets of paper. "What's a normal temperature?" I questioned, probing for the reason for Carol's "hmm." "Thirty-seven degrees Celsius is 98.6 degrees Fahrenheit; she's pretty cool and has been for a while now. We added more clothes and upped the temp in the incubator this morning, but she's still cold."

After doing some blood work, the doctors found that Ella's red blood cell count was low again. Her body was reproducing red blood cells at a good speed, but wasn't fast enough to catch her up to where she needed to be, which was causing her to have a low body temperature. The doctor told me, "Her body just can't maintain itself yet; just another side effect of being a preemie." A second blood transfusion was the answer to the problem. So again, I watched as blood was pumped into my tiny babe. This roller coaster of NICU life was at times disheartening. Ella seemed to be progressing to health so quickly, but then, we'd get these reminders of how her time on this earth began, and that her life was indeed still very fragile.

17

Belief

"ARE YOU SURE YOU AREN'T going to leave the room for this?" The nurse asked me. A week before, they had checked Ella's eyes as Calvin stayed calmly by Ella's side, and found that Ella had some concerning blood vessels in her right eye. I had been in another room pumping during that first exam, and now, as I watched the procedure, I could see why it was common for the parents to step out.

The pediatric ophthalmologist numbed Ella's eyes first with drops, which Ella didn't much care for, and then used a metal scissor-like tool that slid in between her eyelids to hold them apart. At this, Ella screamed at the top of her lungs. A month ago while Ella was unconscious and depending on life support to sustain her, when not a peep was heard from my girl, I would have done anything to hear sound come from her mouth, *any* sound; but now, it ripped my heart out as I watched helplessly from the sidelines as the doctor rolled Ella's eyeball with a spoon-like scoop from one side to the other while carefully inspecting it.

A bright light positioned on the doctor's head, much like a miner's lamp, shone into the lens of Ella's dilated eye, allowing the doctor to see any disease or disfigurement that may have occurred from the many weeks of high oxygen levels. This went on for several minutes. I stood stoically at the head of Ella's bed, even helping to keep her hands away from the instruments while she struggled and screamed, but inside I was like a dam at maximum capacity, about ready to burst at the sight of my poor baby in pain, and powerless to stop it. Tears of blood rolled from Ella's eyes and spilled upward and onto her cap, staining it with spots of crimson as her head was tilted back so that the doctor had a good angle to inspect.

When the heart-wrenching ordeal was finally over, a new, devastating diagnosis was delivered by Ella's ophthalmologist, Dr. White. "Ella has a disease in her eyes called retinopathy of prematurity. She will need surgery right away. Right now, the blood vessels that nourish her eyes have been fed way too much oxygen and have started to creep up into the gel space of the eye, pulling the retina up with them. If the retinas fully detach, she will go blind. So, we'll plan to do laser surgery tomorrow to try and zap all of those wayward blood vessels that are pulling the retina away from its position and hope that it fixes the problem." She said this very matter-of-factly as her lips flatly lined up, like she was saying, "We'll shoot for the best, but my hopes aren't real high."

So much had happened in the past few weeks that it was hard to believe that Ella was now facing losing her eyesight. I mentally scanned the last few days and recalled how Ella had come off of the CPAP breathing device and had been "promoted" to a nasal cannula, just a tiny little hose with two prongs fitting into the nostrils that connects any typical hospital patient to oxygen. What a *huge* milestone, since Ella had been diagnosed with hypoplastic lungs at birth and had required pressurized oxygen for the first 35 days of her life!

Continuing to marvel at Ella's progress, I remembered how Ella had moved from recreational breast-feeding (nursing from my freshly-pumped breast just to practice, so as not to choke on a heavy flow of milk) to actually nursing for nourishment, with less and less of her milk given through the feeding tube! In fact, since the blood transfusion, Ella had become a new baby entirely. She no longer needed the incubator bed to keep warm and was promoted to a crib. She was on hardly any medication, which was simply a miracle considering that only a short month earlier, she'd been on life support, depending completely on machines and medicines to keep her entire body functioning! It seemed that every day a different doctor or nurse would come into Ella's room and tell us how well Ella was doing.

I recalled one nurse named Sunshine who came in one day, and astonished at the progress that Ella was making said, "Wow. I just don't know how this is possible!" That same day, another nurse popped her head in, as many nurses made a habit of doing during the day just to check on the little miracle, Baby Wilkins, and after discovering Ella's amazing status said, "She's light-years ahead of where I thought she'd be!"

A few short hours later, Ella's primary doctor, a neonatologist named Dr. Zara (the same doctor who predicted that Ella would probably never be born alive) came around to stop by Ella's bed. As he looked her over, checked her vitals and her chart, a large grin spread widely across his face and then he spoke with absolute amazement, "She looks good, doesn't she?" Beaming, his eyes met mine. "It's a miracle," I said, so choked up those were the only words I could get out. "Yes, we are happy," he replied. For Dr. Zara to be *that* pleased with Ella's progress was huge, because I considered him to be one of the more cautious and conservative neonatologists on the team when it came to optimism.

Yes, it was clear; our Ella was doing outstandingly better than she ever should have. This new diagnosis for her eyes was just a drop in the bucket, and we'd take the news in stride.

Snapped back to the moment by something the doctor was saying, I was overcome with faith and said to the ophthalmologist, "God has brought this little baby girl a long way. He's working miracles in her life and I'm going to pray that her eyes will be healed and she won't need this surgery tomorrow." A strange look stretched across Dr. White's face, a look very similar to the look my OB specialist had given me when I told him that God was in charge of my life and the baby's and that we would not have an abortion. It was almost as if she had pity for this ignorant little mommy who had no understanding whatsoever of medical realities.

With a sarcastic laugh, she said, "Well, I think you should just pray that the surgery goes well, because she *needs* it." Holding my position with a broad smile on my lips, I said, "I'll be praying that you'll be pleasantly surprised tomorrow by not needing to do the surgery." Without missing a beat and with sarcasm in her voice, Dr. White replied, "OK," and with another half smile and nod of her head, she exited the room. When she was gone, Ella's nurse, Darla, who had previously been very pessimistic about Ella's conditions, came up to me and whispered, "I'll be praying for Ella too."

Adrenaline and excitement laced my veins as I imagined the doctor checking Ella's eyes in the morning and discovering complete healing! If I'd learned anything from my time on bed rest, it's that God wants us to believe when we ask Him to do something, and I believed that He'd heal my baby daughter's eyes. The doctor would be so surprised! And with the extent of her skepticism and sarcasm concerning the reality of a god, I just knew that *this* could be the point at which she realized that God exists!

With excitement still rushing through my body, I quickly found a phone and called everyone I could think of to ask them for prayer. My first phone call was to my dad. I asked him to bring Grandpa Bob and our beloved senior pastor, Kent Conrad, to pray over Ella and anoint her in Jesus' name. I had seen many miracles and huge obstacles overcome by the power of prayer, and this surgery on Ella's eyes seemed worthy of some intense prayer. I continued making phone calls until my list was exhausted, and then I dropped to my knees and began praying for the healing of Ella's eyes. Praises and thanksgiving arose from my lips to the throne of our God Almighty for the miracles He had performed in our little baby's life. My request for healing on Ella's eyes was almost a statement instead of a question as I prayed with certainty and complete belief that God would provide ultimate healing, and thanked Him in advance for the work He was going to do in Ella's body.

Later that evening, my dad, Grandpa Bob, and Pastor Conrad arrived to pray over my sweet babe. After scrubbing in, the four of us gathered around Ella's crib in the NICU. Then, I lifted Ella out and handed her to my dad. This was first time he'd ever had the privilege of holding her. "She's so tiny," he whispered, a bright and toothy grin stretching across his face as he carefully studied his miniature granddaughter. As we huddled in a tight circle and bowing our heads, Pastor Conrad asked earnestly for God's will and for healing over Ella's eyes as he anointed her head with oil. He had such a way of communicating with the Creator of our universe, and I was so thankful that he had come.

**Pastor Conrad; my dad, Jeff, holding Ella and my
grandpa, Bob; the night they prayed over Ella's eyes.**

Pastor Conrad had been such a source of encouragement to me during
this whole ordeal. He and his sweet wife, Kay, had come to visit and pray
with me while I was on bed rest a few different times. Among his many acts
of love and selflessness, he had come and helped me label my groceries and
put them away in the storage cabinets where I was staying at the Ronald
McDonald house before joining me in the NICU to pray over a week-old
Ella. He was a man who loved the Lord and loved God's people. And now,
as he prayed and anointed my sweet baby, I was so touched by his faith
and willingness to serve, even late at night! What a powerful moment to
be a part of!

When we were finished praying, I realized that Ella's nurse, Darla, had
been in the room for the sweet time of prayer and seemed to be curiously
observing our little group. It was in that moment that I prayed for her soul
and that she'd be touched by this experience.

After saying good-bye to these wonderful men of God and kissing
our sweet Ella goodnight, I made my way to my room at the Ronald
McDonald house. Sitting on my bed with my face freshly washed, I

penned a passage in my journal. The words flowed from my mind and onto the pages as peace and excitement filled my spirit. The entry ended with these last few sentences of faith and determination that I now find interesting to reread:

> *"Now, I just can't wait for tomorrow to see Dr. White's [Ella's eye doctor's] expression when she checks Ella's eyes! I am so excited I can't sleep! Praise God! The maker and creator! He made Ella in the first place, why can't He heal her eyes!?!"*

....

Journal entry the day of Ella's eye surgery, June 19, 2008:

> *"This life is so curious. Just when you think you have it all figured out, God throws a curveball. It's not necessarily a bad thing, just not what you expected. When I was pregnant with Ella, I felt a push from God to go out on a limb and* believe *in the fact that God was going to save her little life. And boy does it take some energy to really believe in the midst of waiting. But when I finally got to the point of being bold about this faith, God decides He wants to teach me another lesson . . . that His plan is perfect.*
>
> *"Ella had laser surgery on her eyes today. What a shock that was for me. I believed with my whole heart that God would heal her eyes. That this would be the perfect miracle to perform to show His awesome power and glory to the doctors and nurses. But God had a different plan. He allowed the surgery to take place. It kind of knocked the wind out of me at first. I was so sure God wanted to show His power in an obvious way, but I didn't bother to ask Him. I just assumed. My prayer should have been, 'Lord, use this situation and possible surgery to your glory in whichever way you see fit, and use me to shine your light.' I mean, since when did I start giving orders to God as to how He was going to show His power?*
>
> *"So now, I am very interested to see how He is going to use this. We will never understand the mind of God. And we are never done learning. Just when we have a revelation, He shows us He is bigger. He*

humbles us, in a way. I need a lot of humbling. I love God so much. His is my king. I need to remember that He sees the big picture and I only see a fraction.

"Ella's surgery did go well. We won't know until next week what effect it's had on her eyes. Now, I will sit back, hand it over to Jesus, and watch the story unfold."

．．．．．．．．．．．．．．．．．．．．．

Watching Calvin hold our tiny babe after she was delivered to us from surgery was a very beautiful and private moment. His arms looked massive in comparison with Ella's tiny form, and again, I was reminded of the greatness of our God! He had allowed us to receive this amazing little gift and was carrying each member of our family through this time of devastation and miracles. Together, Calvin and I gazed down at our little miracle child who was going through more than most people ever experience in a lifetime, and she wasn't even supposed to be born yet. We were given instructions to keep the bandages on her eyes and to keep a cool-pack on them to help with recovery from her surgery. With heavy hearts, Cal and I cuddled our precious girl and whispered softly to her as she began to wake up and realize discomfort and a very different world.

18

Never Say Never

Two days before Ella's eye surgery, the head nurse had come into Ella's hospital room and said to her, "How do you do without your nasal cannula?" as she pulled the tiny tubes from Ella's nostrils and unwound the tubing from behind the ears, leaving her completely devoid of oxygen assistance. Panic rose in my chest the instant the prongs were pulled from Ella's nose; it was as if a thousand fire crackers were going off inside of me, and it was all I could do to keep the signs of smoke from coming out of my mouth and nose. The nurse had seemed so casual as she removed the life-saving gas from my baby, but then, I could see that she was watching Ella's monitor closely for dips in heart rate or oxygen level in her blood.

At first, Ella had dipped down into the 70s, and anyone who's spent any time in the NICU with a baby who has trouble keeping oxygen levels up knows that's when the baby's coloring starts to gray and darken, while alarms next to the bed ding at a faster pace and heighten until they're silenced or there's some sort of improvement. Slowly though, Ella's coloring started to even out and her oxygen levels started coming up. Never, ever do I wish to repeat those minutes of waiting for Ella's oxygen levels to resurge and reach 100 percent.

Eventually though, Ella did learn to breathe effectively and maintain a healthy level of oxygenation without the help of a nasal cannula. The eye surgery had, however, caused Ella to be re-intubated (put back on the ventilator), but as soon as the surgery was over, the vent was removed

121

and she wore the nasal cannula for a day until her body woke up enough to effectively process oxygen again. It was a step backwards, and in the process of trying to hit milestones in order to be released to go home, any backwards movement was unwelcome. But in light of Ella's "course," it had been a miracle for her to have only required extra oxygen the day of the surgery! Yes, she had taken a step backward, but only momentarily, and it was completely evident that the Creator of the universe was the one caring for our little girl.

....

Placing Ella back into the crib after the physical therapist was finished, I just stared at our girl, amazed at how she had defied the odds. The doctors had said that she would be born dead. And yes, she was born lifeless, but now she's alive! The doctors also said she'd have terrible bone contractures because of the weight of my uterus that had crushed her, and she did have bone contractures in her arms and legs at birth, but now, our physical therapist had just informed us that there was not a single contracture remaining and that Ella's bones looked completely normal!

Our nurse, Darla, approached me then. She was the nurse who had been present the night we had anointed Ella with oil and prayed over her, and who had previously been very pessimistic about Ella's conditions and forthright about ignoring my comments about God. But now she came to me and said, "Ella should not be here right now. For her bones to be so straight and healing so rapidly," she took a deep breath then and exhaled slowly, "There's someone else you need to thank." Her eyes stared deeply into mine, revealing that she'd finally "bought into" belief in this God of ours and could no longer ignore the great work He was doing in our baby's life.

....

Nearing the end of June, we were finally informed that Ella had made enough progress to take steps towards the possibility of taking her home. She was finally getting most of her nourishment from breast-feeding and only a tiny portion from the feeding tube. Along with feeding improvements, Ella was maintaining a healthy body temperature and was slowly gaining weight. Also, Ella had not received any oxygen assistance in a week! All of these improvements were criteria to be able to go home. Only a few obstacles remained: Ella needed to pass the car seat study and she needed to continue growing even after removing the feeding tube. So it was determined that I would move over to the hospital and stay in one of the parent rooms in order to breast-feed Ella around the clock, to make sure that she could still grow and thrive without the use of her feeding tube.

Before, when I was staying at the Ronald McDonald house, I'd freeze and store the breast milk from my middle-of-the-night pumping sessions and then bring them to the NICU for the nurses to use at night, either in a bottle or feeding tube, depending on if Ella was having a good day or bad day. Now, however, they wanted Ella in a clear pattern of healthy eating to be sure she could handle life at home without a feeding tube. The car seat study was scheduled for two days later, and I made plans to leave my room at the Ronald McDonald house and sign into the hospital's parent room.

....

After a grueling 90 minutes in the car seat, the results were in; Ella failed. Her oxygen levels had bounced around and were significantly affected by the unusual angle of the car seat. The low oxygen saturation in Ella's blood was not the only red flag sent up by the study; Ella also experienced bradycardia (a slow or dipping heart rate). With this new information, the car seat study was rescheduled for another day, and the journey home was set back yet again.

....

The days following the failed car seat study seemed endless, with grueling around-the-clock feedings. I had to walk through the endless, cold halls of the hospital from my parent room to the NICU, scrub in, and make my way to Ella's hospital room three times a night. Maneuvering around cords and wires that were still attached to Ella's body also made for less sleep and added time to nightly feeds.

After three or four nights of successful breast-feeding, the doctors decided it would be OK to move Ella to my parent room. Along with Ella came her rolling crib, medical equipment, alarms, and more. I was told to treat this time of having her in my room as normal as possible, but if at any time I needed a nurse, I could just hit my call button and someone would join me as soon as possible. The nurse who moved Ella to my room assured me that they would be watching Ella's monitor, and if an alarm went off in my room, she would be able to hear it at her station as well. Calvin made arrangements to come and help me take shifts caring for Ella.

And I thought sleeping with a newborn who wakes up frequently to eat was tiring! Waking up with each alarm, plus the feeds, without the expertise of the doctors and nurses, was even more exhausting and nerve-racking. After three successful nights of "parent watch" with lots of help from Calvin, we were both sufficiently tired, but Ella had made great strides in the right direction and hadn't required even one feed from the tube. Things were starting to look up.

....

By the time we had come upon the next car seat study, I felt like a walking zombie and wasn't sure how much longer I'd be able to continue on in this manner. Including the time I was on bed rest in the hospital, I had been away from home, Calvin, and Ariana for over three months, and my energy and stamina were beginning to fade. It was my deepest prayer that Ella would pass this car seat study and be able to come home.

As Ella slept in her car seat, I sat quietly next to her and tried to read my Bible. After several minutes of being unable to focus on what I was reading because of my nerves, I decided that I had to escape to a spot where I wasn't just staring at the monitors and wondering if Ella would pass *this* study.

With Bible in hand, I made my way through the work stations of the NICU, when one of the respiratory therapists stopped me. He was a tall man with a salt-and-pepper goatee, and with an almost surprised look on his face, he said, "We knew there was something different about you guys!" For an instant I was confused, until I noticed him pointing to my Bible. He continued, "We knew there was *something* different, now we know what the difference is!" The sentence flowed from his mouth with a wink and a smile, and then he continued, "It's obvious to everyone around you, keep it up."

God had just sent me encouragement in the form of a respiratory therapist! The thought that God's light was shining through our family and that it was *obvious* to everyone around us was deeply gratifying and humbling. I knew that if left to our own devices, we would have screwed the whole thing up, but with God's amazing love, provision, and ability to carry us through the darkest and most exhausting times I had ever known, He shown brightly! Wow. That was more than I could have ever asked for.

> "Come to me, all you who are weary and
> burdened, and I will give you rest."
>
> ❧ MATTHEW 11:28

....

Riding the wheelchair on our way out of the hospital with Ella tucked safely into her car seat on my lap was so surreal. I honestly felt like a doctor would come running after us with arms waving in the air, screaming, "Wait! Wait! We found another problem. You can't go!" But no such doctor came. I felt a little silly in the wheelchair because it had been so long since my C-section, but it was hospital protocol, so I abided by the rules. Whatever it took to get to go home, I would do it. As we rolled down the familiar hallways toward the freedom that beckoned from outside the rotating doors, I couldn't help but to feel a little bit scared and really alone. Physically, emotionally, and spiritually I was not alone, for I had Calvin by my side, Jesus in my heart, and an entire family and church full of friends who all wanted to help, but we were leaving without monitors! With Ella's passed car seat study, a flood of relief had come over me, but as soon as it dawned on me that we would be going home without the doctors, nurses, and medical equipment, I started to feel a bit apprehensive.

You might think I'm crazy that I wanted to bring home dinging alarms and monitors, but anyone who has ever taken a baby home after having the comfort of knowing that if the slightest problem occurred, a sensor would pick it up, knows how insecure I was feeling at that moment. I had spent the last two weeks studying Ella so that I would be able to recognize just by looking at her coloring about what number her oxygen level was, but with all the time spent learning, I still felt nervous about the night hours when my eyes would not be glued on Ella.

What if she stopped breathing? What if her heart rate dropped? What if? What if? What if? Again, the "what ifs" tried to overtake me. Wrangling my thoughts to another direction and trying to ignore the worries and lies that the evil one would have me focus on, a new set of positive thoughts took hold of me.

We were *finally* going home to live for the first time as a family! Yes, it would be new to live at home with both of my girls and without alarms, but also liberating and amazing! After 50 long days in the NICU, we were on our way home and experiencing yet another miracle, for Ella was not coming home with *any* medication. Let me repeat, she was not on *any* medication whatsoever! And as I stated before, she wasn't using any monitors, either.

It was so unbelievable that somewhere there needed to be a catch. How could a baby who was born basically dead, then was resuscitated, was diagnosed with lung disease and pulmonary hypertension, just avoided kidney failure, had one (possibly two) brain bleeds and dangerously low blood pressure, experienced two blood transfusions, and encountered many other life-threatening ailments, now be leaving the hospital in record time with no medications? That, my friends, is called a miracle!

Ella had been cleared to go and was sent home before her estimated due date of July 17! In fact, she had beat the date by almost a month, going home on June 26, at only 37 weeks gestational age and weighing in at 4 pounds 11 ounces!

I was thankful now that I had heard God's voice all those weeks ago and believed Him! When the challenge had come to prepare my fields for rain, some had thought I was crazy, just as the people in Bible times had thought Noah was when he was building the ark. But in the end, Noah and I both ended up sopping wet from God's outpouring of blessing! I had prepared my fields for the rain, and when it came, I was able to reap a harvest!

"Jesus replied, 'I tell you the truth, if you have faith and do not doubt, not only can you do what was done to the fig tree, but also you can say to this mountain, "Go, throw yourself into the sea," and it will be done. If you believe, you will receive whatever you ask for in prayer.'"

ชม MATTHEW 21:21-22

"And without faith it is impossible to please God, because anyone who comes to him must believe that he exists and that he rewards those who earnestly seek him."

ชม HEBREWS 11:6

19

Portland Oregon

BEING READMITTED TO ANOTHER NICU only two weeks after being discharged from the hospital was like being weighed down with a ton of bricks. Upon departure from Ella's first hospital stay, we were given some information that had brought us to this current location, Portland, Oregon. Dr. White had informed us that the laser surgery she performed on Ella's little eyes had not been effective, and the disease in Ella's eyes was progressing rapidly and needed immediate surgery to try to prevent blindness. She sent us to a pediatric specialist, Dr. Short, who performed a surgery called a vitrectomy.

Before the surgery, Dr. Short explained to us that Ella's optical blood vessels were growing so wildly that they were pulling the retina away, and in fact, both retinas were almost completely detached, leaving her without vision for the time being. With this surgery, the vitrectomy, Dr. Short believed that he might be able to cause the retinas to lay back into place by removing all the gel-like substance from both eyes.

By removing the substance that the blood vessels were clinging to, he believed the newly relaxed vessels would allow the retinas to be released into their correct positions. Once the retinas were relaxed, he would refill her eyes with a new solution that would not provide as much traction for those vessels to cling to.

"There's no guarantee that Ella will ever have vision again, even with this surgery," Dr. Short reminded us before the procedure. "It's just a step to try and see what we come out with. Sometimes it works and sometimes it doesn't. Ella's eyes have rapidly deteriorated, but I think this is the best procedure for her," he finished.

It was sort of an eerie feeling to be getting our girl ready for the second surgery of her life two weeks before she was even due to be born. I knew the surgery had to take place and be done right away, but everything about sending my newborn baby off to be put under anesthesia and cut on again seemed wrong. Mothers of infants are usually never more than a few steps away from them, and I was learning how to deal with distances and complete helplessness. It was in these moments that Cal and I would turn to prayer.

As the nurses were finishing up their pre-op preparations, Calvin and I took a moment to pray over our girl before they took her off for surgery. I didn't close my eyes as Cal prayed, and I'll never forget the sight of her in his arms. He held our little Ella in his large hands, and with his head bowed above hers, he poured out his heart to our God, asking that He'd keep her safe and work miracles in her life. I don't remember all of his words, but I remember how the moment felt. It was just the most humbling, beautiful thing to watch as this big man whom I loved so much prayed so helplessly over his sweet child. And as he prayed, drops of water fell from his eyes onto Ella's miniature hospital gown. The sight of this mighty man of God, praying so fervently over the tiny, wiggling bundle in his arms, continues to be one of my most precious memories.

....

During the surgery, Calvin and I walked the length of the balcony at the Portland hospital and stood quietly in each other's presence. I remember pausing at one point while we both rested our elbows and forearms on the ledge of the balcony wall with the vast view of the city stretched out below. Side by side we stared off into the breeze, allowing the sun to kiss our faces as we waited and wondered what God had planned for our girl.

While we waited, my mind returned to the moment we had brought Ella home from the hospital. Ari and my mom had been waiting at our house for us to arrive. We had thought it would be good for Ariana to be there waiting rather than to have her come home to find her daddy, mommy, and little sister already there. We wondered if it would be confusing to her, like maybe we had been there all along and she'd been staying with her grandparents. I'm so glad we had her waiting for us because it kind of put her in "hostess" mode.

As soon as we walked in, she was there to greet her new baby sister. I asked Ariana to show Ella around the house, so Ari had the privilege of introducing her new sibling to her world. What a special day it had been to finally relax and spend time together as a complete family in our own home! Four and a half months had passed from the time my water broke to the day we brought Ella home from the hospital, so "normal" moments together as a family were now greatly cherished.

With my mind on Ariana, my heart gave a jolt as new pain seeped from my innermost being, for Calvin and I were missing out on being with her again. We had taken this trip to Portland the day before her second birthday and left her at home with my parents. Being away from Ari never got easy; even after all the time I had spent in Boise away from her, I only craved time with her more. But our trip to Portland was urgent and greatly needed for the sake of Ella's vision. We had met with Ella's surgeon on Ariana's birthday, while her grandmothers took her out for a special birthday lunch at her favorite fast-food joint.

We really do have the best family in the whole wide world. How many grandmothers from either side of the family get together to do special things for their grandchildren? It definitely helps that my mom has been acquainted with Calvin's mom, Jill, since before I was born and that there is a long history of friendship between the two families. I knew that Ariana was well cared for, but it still didn't make up for the sickening feelings of "missing out" that I had. I loved that little girl more than anything, and it felt so wrong to be away from her!

....

The surgery lasted three hours. Dr. Short had found us waiting on the balcony and announced that the surgery had gone well, but we wouldn't have results on her vision for a few weeks. He directed us back to Ella's

NICU room where she was waiting for us. Once in the room, a faint cry coming from Ella's hospital bed drew Calvin and me to her side. The NICU rooms here were much different than the ones in Boise. Here, the floors were tiled rather than carpeted, beds were closer together with one nurse tending to four or five babies, but on the bright side (literally), these rooms had large windows that let in all the sunshine that the Boise hospital had not.

As Cal and I quickly moved to Ella's side, it was hard to control the emotions of utter pity that overtook us as we watched Ella swiping at the bandages over her eyes with her equally bandaged hands. She had given the nurses a challenge again when they tried to start her IV, so Band–Aids spotted one hand and arm representing missed attempts, while the other hand with the IV displayed extensive tape and colorful wrap to keep it securely fastened. As Ella came out from under the anesthesia, she became more and more uncomfortable with all of her restraints.

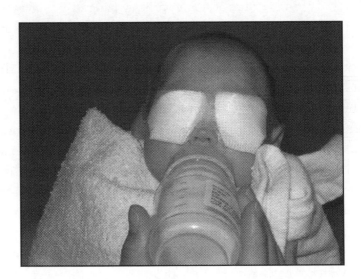

This is Ella when she took her first feed after her eye surgery.

Dr. Short had recommended that we leave the bandages on her eyes for the time being to allow for maximum healing. I imagined that Ella was probably feeling confused and disoriented, unable to see what was going on around her because of the mysterious coverings over her eyes. Seeing

Ella with bandages over her eyes and realizing just how serious her vision problem was, Calvin and I had to start to come to terms with the fact that we might be raising a blind child.

....

It seemed like much more than a week had passed since we arrived back home from Portland. So much had happened. In that week, we had thrown a last-minute party for Ariana's second birthday, home-made cake and all, cared for Ella with her new routine of eye drops and pain killers, and run to daily doctor appointments to follow up on several of Ella's previous ailments. We visited four different doctors' offices in just one week. Exhaustion was my ever-present companion, with waking up for Ella's nightly feedings, and then again with Arana in between the feedings because she hadn't yet adjusted to being back home.

Calvin was still working the very early morning shift at the food service, which meant that he was off-limits for baby duty at night to ensure that he would not be sleepy while he drove his large semi truck at work. So I had the brunt of the sleepless nights, which made things a little tricky when I had to get myself and two kids ready (fed, dressed, diapers changed, bags packed, car loaded, and kids buckled up) and to the appointments on time!

One of the appointments we had gone to that week was a follow-up on Ella's brain bleed that she had experienced at birth. The technician performed an ultrasound on her head that exposed great pictures of her brain. At that appointment, the doctor had told us that the blood was still sitting in the brain, but didn't look like it was causing any problems and that it would probably absorb into the body within a matter of months. It was a great relief to find out that Ella's brain bleed wasn't throwing up any immediate red flags, but the stress that came from trying to keep a two-year-old away from buttons and a wiggly baby secure on the table with only two arms left me frazzled and ready for a nap.

Another appointment we had gone to that week was for an echocardiogram. Just before Ella had been discharged from the hospital in Boise, the doctors had found a clot in her heart. The clot originated while Ella had been in the hospital during the first days of her life. The doctor had threaded lines and tubes through Ella's belly button and up through a main vessel in her tummy to an area near her heart to allow for medications and nutrition to be distributed throughout the body. But the lines had somehow gone farther than was safe and moved in and through Ella's right chamber of her heart and into the left chamber, which does the high-pressure pumping of blood to the body.

After inserting these lines, doctors always follow up with X-rays to make sure the position of the lines are acceptable, and in the first few days, Ella's X-rays showed that the lines were correctly situated. But sometime after that, the lines had adjusted and moved into the dangerous left chamber of the heart.

While resting in Ella's heart, the tube attracted particles from Ella's body that formed a cast around the tube, which remained in Ella's heart once the tube was removed. The doctors had caught sight of the cast on an ultrasound right before she'd been discharged. They weren't too concerned because normally these small particle build-ups break down and disperse, but because it was in the left side of Ella's heart, they wanted to make sure to keep an eye on it.

After the echo, we were introduced to Ella's pediatric cardiologist, Dr. Argon. "I'm incredibly concerned about this cast in your daughter's heart," she started. "Not only is the cast still there, but it has grown significantly since the last ultrasound." Dr. Argon's head dropped for a moment as she seemed to be searching for words, and then she raised her head and locked eyes with me, "The neonatologists scheduled this appointment as a precautionary measure, but had not expected the cast to grow. I need to do some research and find out what would be a safe way to treat such a small baby." She stopped then, her dark eyes looking beyond me, deep in thought, "I think she needs to be anticoagulated, but I don't think they make a dose small enough for Ella. I'll have to call you with what I find."

I just stood there trying to pretend like I understood what the doctor was telling me. Could Ella really have a dangerous clot in her heart? I had so many questions swirling around in my brain and yet had been told to wait because the doctors did not have the answers. Why did Ella seem to be the baby without a manual, the one who broke all the medical trends? Or so it seemed to me.

Not only had Ella needed the standard eye surgery required for retinopathy of prematurity, but she had also needed a reconstructive eye surgery that we had to travel to Portland for, and now . . . now, she had a clot in her heart that the doctors didn't even know how to treat? Questions pulsed through my mind after the appointment as we waited for the phone call that would hopefully deliver answers.

Yes, it had been a busy week, and I only mentioned two of the four appointments that had been on the calendar. I guess I had been wrong when I assumed that life would go back to normal once Ella was discharged from the NICU. What *was* "normal"? Would we ever know "normal," or life as we once knew it, again? We had reached July 17, Ella's due date, and already Ella had almost three months of life outside the womb under her belt. But things were definitely not getting easier.

20

"Normal"

One short day after our trip to the pediatric cardiologist, we heard back from Dr. Argon with some answers. She explained to me over the phone that she had consulted two reliable sources to gain more information on Ella's condition and what the proper treatment should be. The first group of specialists that Dr. Argon spoke with was a cluster of physicians located in Canada who deal especially with blood clots in the heart. She also gained information from some very prestigious pediatric cardiologists in Portland, Oregon to help come up with a treatment plan especially for Ella. During our phone conversation, Dr. Argon reiterated to me the fact that Ella's clot was very concerning and would be life-threatening if it went untreated, causing either a stroke or heart failure.

"Do you think the research you found and treatment plan you decided on will be effective?" I questioned as the familiar feeling of panic began to rise in my chest. I couldn't imagine coming this far, finally feeling somewhat secure with Ella's more severe ailments falling off the radar screen, only to lose her because of a heart attack. My breathing quickened and I willed myself to calm down. I knew I needed to hear all of what Dr. Argon had to say, and so I tried to focus.

"Well, it's our hope that the treatment plan is effective. Ella is definitely a special case and is carrying lots of risks, but I do think that we found a good solution for treatment." When Dr. Argon paused, I took a deep breath in to try and ready myself to hear the treatment plan.

"With the information and research that I gained from the pediatric cardiologist specialists in Oregon and the clot people in Canada, we decided to put Ella on a regimented dose of blood thinners that will hopefully cause the clot to break down slowly and then safely pass through the body. But in order to give a small enough dose, because Ella is still so small, we'll have to give the medication through a subcutaneous injection twice a day for at least three months and possibly up to half a year."

Trying to sort out the information that had just flooded my brain, I started to dissect the doctor's instructions aloud, "OK, so, Ella will need two shots a day?" I asked a little shakily, wondering how in the world that would work. We already had several appointments a week; I couldn't imagine two a day! "Yes, a nurse will actually come to your house and teach you how to give the shots. It's subcutaneous, which means that you won't inject into the muscle, just fatty tissue, so it's pretty simple."

....

"Are you kidding me?" I thought as I was being taught how to give my tiny daughter a shot. The nurse had come by our house to teach me how to give injections and also to deliver the syringes, medical waste box that the used syringes would go into, medical gauze, and alcohol wipes. My mind repeated the steps as the nurse had taught them, "Just hold the syringe like a pencil and go in at an angle, press the medicine into the skin and remove the needle . . ." Those were the words the nurse had used as she demonstrated in the air going into a pretend person.

"Yeah right! First of all, I hate needles and can't even watch a fake injection on TV! How am I supposed to give one?" my mind reeled. "OK, OK," I calmed myself, preparing to insert the needle into a fold of skin on Ella's upper thigh. "You can do this, you can do this, you can do this," I silently encouraged myself over and over. But the longer I sat there staring at the skin pinched between my fingers and the needle in my other hand, the more blurry my vision became and the more shaky my hand got. Finally, the nurse asked if I'd like to watch her do it first and then she could come by that evening and instruct me through the second dose. Relieved, I let the oxygen escape my lugs and shoulders fall from their uptight and stiff position, "Yes, would that be OK?" I pleaded. "Of course, it's not every day someone asks you to learn to give a shot," she said with compassion and a kind grin as she flawlessly gave Ella her first dose of blood thinners.

....

Hidden away on bed rest, I had so desperately missed the sun that was now beating down on my sundress-exposed shoulders. Even in the near 100-degree heat, I was not wishing it cooler; I just enjoyed the hot beams of sun on my skin. My cousin, Tyler was getting married in a beautiful outdoor ceremony in early August that became our first real family outing since Ella had been born in May. Ariana was the flower girl, wearing a sunny peach-colored dress and sporting bare feet as she sort of searched her way to the front of the aisle. At two years old, she was so cute and perfect for the role of a flower girl. Wisps of soft, blond natural curls floated from her head and framed a sun-kissed face as her deep brown eyes hunted for the direction in which she was supposed to go. I don't think she dropped a single flower petal, but she was completely adorable as she made her way to the front and met my cousin Alyssia, the groom's sister and bridesmaid, who enticed her with some chocolate to get her to stand in her spot. Ella's car seat carrier sat at my feet in the grass as she slept soundly in her shaded spot during the ceremony. Tyler married a beautiful girl, Brianne, who just happened to be the daughter of the valley's most well-known news anchor, so the news cameras rolled, it seemed, from every direction, capturing all the special moments of the day. It was indeed a special day, one free of worries, time spent with family, and best of all, no doctor's appointments—just the way I liked it.

....

As August was coming to a close, I started to find my own niche in my new game of life. Ella had anywhere from two to five doctor's appointments every week and was still receiving two injections each day for the clot in her heart. Ariana was learning to find fun ways to pass the time in waiting rooms and doctor's offices, and I was getting better at managing two kids simultaneously. Even after almost two months at home, life had not gone back to normal, but I was beginning to come to terms with the fact that it probably never would and I needed to embrace my new way of life.

A good friend of mine, Sarah LeBaron, had taught me that sometimes we need to surrender our old idea of "normal" and embrace the new "normal." Having grown up on the mission field and now juggling being the wife of our children's pastor and mothering three children of her own, Sarah knew a bit about living with inconsistencies. She frequently checked in on me because she knew how crazy life was for us with Calvin only available for family time between three o'clock in the afternoon when he got home from work until six o'clock when he went to bed in the evening, so she'd often ask if I needed a meal, or if she could take Ari to give me a break. Sometimes she'd offer to come and put the kids in bed for me, and other times she just asked if I needed someone to talk to or cry with. I don't know if I would have made it through some of those days if it wasn't for her help and shoulder to cry on. And with her constant encouragement and the grace of Jesus, I was learning to live with our new sense of normal.

....

One evening as I was holding Ella, I looked into her eyes and noticed that I could still see the tiny purple stitches that had sewn her eyeballs back up after her Portland surgery. We still didn't know anything conclusive about her eyesight, just that the vessels in her eyes were behaving themselves, but that the detachments of the retinas had caused quite a bit of damage. In those quiet moments on the couch, with Ella tucked into my arms and eyes beginning to get heavy with sleep, I just stared at her, amazed at the miracle God had given to us.

There wasn't a day that went by that we weren't reminded by *something* (injections, doctor's appointments, new diagnosis, etc.) of where Ella's life began. One of the e-mails I had sent to Grandpa Bob explains just how I was feeling at that time:

> *Please pray for Ella. We are getting rather weary, but God is ALWAYS there to pick us up and carry us. I am amazed at the awesome miracle I hold in my arms each day. I was studying Ella's tiny face the other day and just noticed all the almost microscopic blood vessels in her eyelids and was amazed at how God placed each one in the right place in order for her eye to work properly. And as I've learned more about the body*

(medically) and seen procedures such as the cardiogram, it is absolutely UNDENIABLE that there is a creator GOD! We are extravagant beings that were made precisely as God intended us to be. Even WITH flaws, there is no way that even one portion of our detailed body could function based on "the BIG BOOM" accident. God is in everything! I just can't keep it inside. He is so AWESOME!!

....

God's grace continued to surround me and keep me safe from bad news. One such example was the day in late August when we went to a routine pediatrician's appointment. Dr. Stinson, the pediatrician, found that Ella's left hip was dislocating. By that time, I was to the point where I just had to surrender every morning, "God, you know what has to be done for our little Ella now that she's here, just give me the strength to put one foot in front of the other, and in the process, allow me to shine Your light and lead others to You." That was my prayer.

I felt so bad for our pediatrician, though, because when she was checking Ella's hips and heard the popping sound, she looked to me with worried eyes and said, "I'm so sorry." She exhaled a huge breath and continued, "It seems like *everything* happens to *you* guys!" She looked at me with her eyes filled with compassion. "I think Ella has a dislocated hip, I'm so sorry," she said again with defeat, almost like she had caused the problem. "It's not *your* fault!" I tried to comfort her, "We're OK. God has given us this little miracle and everything else . . . " I raised my hands as if giving it to God, "He'll take care of it." My eyes smiled at hers as I continued, "We're just so thankful to have a doctor who can find these things so we can get them taken care of." My heart had been light. I knew that God was using us and if it meant that Ella would get one ailment after another just so we could be around people and shine Jesus' light, God would take care of us above and beyond what we ever thought to be possible. So, I chose, sometimes every second, to look to God and commit everything to Him.

After the X-rays were taken and confirmed that Ella's hip was, indeed, dislocated, Dr. Stinson referred us to an orthopedic surgeon.

Later, as I sat quietly on the couch at home with Ella cuddled up close to my chest, I remembered these events of the day and enjoyed the peace that flowed so freely from my Savior who lived so actively in my heart and life. Every day was an adventure and we never knew quite what to expect, but with Jesus carrying us, we always knew we were safe. And after all, Ella was alive! That alone was all the blessing we needed!

....

The appointment with Ella's orthopedic surgeon came, and with it came a new way of living. Dr. Brody, the orthopedic surgeon, prescribed that Ella wear a full-body harness to put her legs in a better position and encourage her hip to slip back into place and grow correctly. I was told that Ella would wear this harness for two months and be reevaluated again when that time period came to a close. The studies showed that most babies responded well to the harness and didn't need any further care once the two months were up, so we had great hope that if we could get through the next two months, her hip problem would be solved.

After Dr. Brody showed me how to fit Ella into the harness, it was my turn to try. I laid out the little contraption on the exam table and placed Ella on top of it. As I placed my three-month-old daughter's feet into the sock-like straps and pulled the strips of fabric into place alongside each leg, and then pulled the straps along her body and over her shoulder, fastening them into position, I felt helpless for my girl. As soon as Ella felt the restraints in place, the panic in her face and body became evident and she instantly released the proof of her terror with blood-curdling screams.

At only three months old, Ella was still only the size of a newborn, weighing in around nine pounds, but it did not stop her from fighting every inch of the fabric that restrained the majority of her small body. Short, quick kicks shot out from her miniature legs and with her fingers curled into tight fists, she shook her arms in frustration as the redness in her face grew and her raw, newborn cry rang out to prove the alarm she was feeling.

The harness had straps that came over the shoulders and fastened with Velcro to a horizontal cottony band that wrapped around the chest and led to more strips of Velcro straps that ran the length of Ella's little legs and connected to little booties that covered her feet. It was situated in such a way that her feet were pointed out and knees bent so that she was in a frog position and only had full movement of her hands and arms. Of all the things I had been forced to learn to do for or to Ella in the name of medicine, this was by far the worst. After only a few minutes, Ella's cries stopped because her lungs could not support both crying and continuing to supply oxygen to her body, but she was still very noticeably upset.

Learning to give injections had been hard, but now I was getting so good at it, I could do it in her leg while she was sleeping and she wouldn't even wake up. But this, this was different. Putting Ella in this restricting harness was like I was strapping her down, trapping her and not letting her out. How could I let her know that I was doing it because I loved her?

When I left Dr. Brody's office with Ella strapped into her car seat while wearing the harness and screaming at the top of her lungs once again, she struggled and tried to kick off the cage-like suit that she was confined to. It was at this point that I felt my strength give way, and tears spilled down my cheeks as I sobbed all the way home.

Later, when others would see Ella struggling and squeezing her fists in anger and frustration while emitting a scream of panic, some people would try and comfort me with the fact that she wouldn't remember this, but that excuse didn't work for me. "Right now, in this instant, she knows what's going on, but doesn't understand. Kids carry subconscious memories forever and I don't want her to look at me as her captor," my mind would rage, and the helplessness would start all over again.

Many things were different with the hip harness: changing diapers was harder and more complicated because I had to push the diaper tabs under and through harness straps (which was quite a task in the middle of the night), giving shots around the straps was difficult, and having to remove the entire device the few allowed times a week for baths was not a fun experience either. But it was in those moments that I remembered the verse that I had dedicated to memory in the hospital, 1 Thessalonians 5:16-18 (NCV), "Always be joyful. Pray continually, and give thanks whatever happens. This is what God wants for you in Christ Jesus." It wasn't always easy; in fact, it never was. Being joyful went against my very being, especially when I was being forced to put my child in discomfort every hour of every day; but each time I'd pray and hand everything I was going through over to Jesus, a new peace and joy would flood my spirit and things just didn't feel as hopeless as they had before.

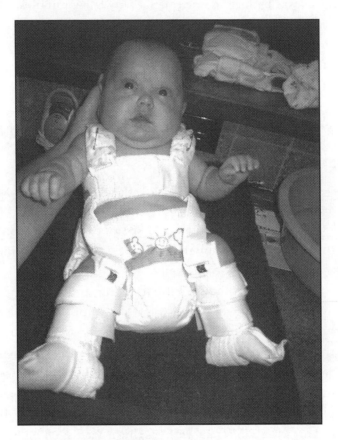

Ella's hip harness.

21

If It Is Going to Happen, It'll Happen to Ella

THE BEGINNING OF OCTOBER 2008 was a joyous time as Ella was released from her harness, but heartbreaking as well because we learned that the harness hadn't been effective and her hip was still dislocated. Dr. Brody told us that Ella would need surgery on her hip in December, followed by three months in a full-body cast.

The two months leading up to Ella's hip surgery were filled with doctor's appointments and planning for my parent's 25th wedding anniversary. We tried our best to enjoy Ella in her freedom before the upcoming cast was applied, but the time went by way too fast.

About two weeks before Ella was scheduled for surgery on her hip, she went in for a scan on her head because it was still very misshapen from being so squished in my stomach. The back right side of her head bulged out while the back left was sunken. Her forehead displayed the same effect. It's a condition called plagiocephaly. After the scan, the doctor advised that we purchase a specially-made helmet that would put equal pressure on all sides of her head and round out the flat spots. But it would not be covered by insurance because the shaping of the head is completely cosmetic.

After much prayer, and advice from family and friends, we decided to go without the helmet and asked the doctor what we could do in place of it. She said that we needed to place all the pressure on the back right side of Ella's head so that the flat left side could push out and become even with the right. The doctor believed creating pressure in that one spot would also cause the sunken left side of Ella's forehead to round out. This may sound like a simple concept, but in reality trying to keep a six-month-old baby's head in a certain position was like trying to play in a pool without getting wet! Keeping correct pressure on Ella's head affected which arm we held her in, where we placed her toys (so that she'd look in a certain direction) and caused us to wake up several times a night to reposition her head and make sure that the pressure was always in the proper spot.

We were more than willing to go to these measures if it saved Ella from having every part of her body receiving some sort of treatment all at once, because if we opted to use the helmet, not only would her head be completely covered, but her torso and legs would be restricted by her upcoming full-body cast, *and* her arms would be receiving the daily shots! Only her feet and hands would go untouched. So, to save Ella from the confines of a helmet, day in and day out we were aware of what position her head was in and where the pressure was being placed. It was incredibly tiring, but we believed that it would all be worth it.

....

The morning of Ella's hip surgery arrived, and the drill was always the same. She was not allowed to "eat" any breast milk eight hours before the surgery, and as with previous operations, she was scheduled as the first surgery of the day because she was typically the youngest of all the patients. Little kids often don't understand why they can't eat for long periods of time, so they take the little ones first. So, our day started bright and early at 5:00 a.m. to make it to the hospital to check in by 6:30.

Once all the consent forms were signed, we were led down to the pre-op room and given a tiny hospital gown for Ella to change into. Once changed and waiting for the nurses to escort Ella to the operating room, I had a chance to just play with Ella. As I looked her over, I could not believe this was the same baby who was rescued from my womb only six months prior. She did not look like a preemie because she wasn't underweight and sickly. Ella was actually quite the opposite.

For the first several months of Ella's life, the pediatrician instructed me to pump my breast milk every three hours and mix it with formula to double Ella's calorie intake to help fatten her up, but after only three months, my pump broke (probably from being used six times a day for three months). At that point, I began exclusively nursing Ella, and when I told the doctor, she feared that Ella would lose weight. As I looked at her now, I could see that gaining weight was not an issue anymore! My mom was even accusing me of making her obese, and had Ella been consuming anything other than breast milk, I might have taken her seriously.

Ella had fat rolls everywhere imaginable. Her little wrists looked as if a rubber band had dipped into her skin and created a fold between her hands and her forearms. I could count at least four rolls on her chubby little legs and three on her arms. Her cheeks were the size of muffins, just hanging off of her face, and in the center was the most adorable little mouth. Her sweet little lips smiled up at me as I continued to inspect her.

She had eyes that lit up at the sound of her mommy's voice, and her nose perfectly dotted the center of her face, not too big and not too small, just right. All of her dark hair from birth had fallen out and light fuzz was beginning to appear on the top of her head. My little baby looked perfect. I was so amazed at the way she had progressed and grown into a healthy baby even without the aid of formula-fortified breast milk! Anyone who saw Ella could tell that she had not recently missed a meal and never would have guessed that she was born prematurely!

The nurse who came in to weigh and check Ella was absolutely mesmerized by her charm. Every time the nurse would bend down and talk to her, Ella's eyes would ignite and she'd smile and coo back at her. When the nurse asked for more information on Ella's medical history, she was astonished at the way Ella's life had begun. Astounded at the story, she asked me, "So, how did they save her?" "Well, they didn't," I said simply, and then added, "Jesus did."

After I concluded the report on Ella's health history up to current time, the nurse lowered to Ella's level on the bed and just looked at her in amazement. "Someone really wanted you here, didn't they?" she whispered to Ella with tear-filled eyes. Ella squealed with delight back at her. Sharing Ella's story with medical people was so rewarding because they could see from a medical point of view how impossible her situation had been and what a miracle her life really was!

Ella continued with her giggling. Even when the nurses were prepping Ella for surgery by getting the IV started, she'd smile at all the nurses in between sobbing from the pokes. It was just as if Jesus was there, holding and comforting her. She was nearly always a happy girl, and I knew that it was not just happiness, but true *joy* that sustained her. With all that Ella had gone through in her extremely young life, to have the absolute joy and peace she exhibited, she had to be being comforted by the Great I Am, the Creator of the universe, our Almighty God! And it was apparent to everyone around her that there was something different about this little baby girl.

....

After Ella had gone for eight hours without food and two hours without liquids, and I had met with the surgeon, anesthesiologist, and nurses and all the pre-op "stuff" was completed, Ella was ready for surgery. There's nothing quite like handing over your child to complete strangers so that she can be cut open and worked on.

This surgery was supposed to be pretty basic. They would go in, cut a ligament that was hindering Ella's femur from properly sitting in the hip socket, set the ball in place, sew her up, put on the cast, and she was done. We were told that the incision was only going to be about a half inch long, so she wouldn't be in too much pain or lose a great deal of blood, but as with any surgery, there was risk of infection or of something going wrong with the anesthesia. For the most part, though, I was at ease. I knew that God had this little girl in His hands. She had only known life on the earth for a little under half a year, but already we had a clear sense that Jesus had special plans for her, and a little ol' surgery wasn't going to mess things up.

....

Everything was perfect. The cake was centered on the table with edible photos of my parents pasted on the icing, the candles were lit, and 25th wedding decorations adorned the living room of my aunt Rhonda Gray's house. She had generously offered to host the party my siblings and I had been secretly planning, and with her help, it looked perfect! Yes, my parent's anniversary party was officially here and everything was going just as planned. Mom and Dad had been thoroughly surprised when we handed them an invitation to their own party while out to lunch that day and they realized that the party started in only 15 minutes. We threw bride and groom hats on them and whisked them off to celebrate their commitment to love each other made 25 years prior.

As guests made their way around the room to grab refreshments and mingle, my mind drifted once again to Ella.

I couldn't help but feel a surge of disappointment with the fact that Ella had to repeat her hip surgery and start the 3 month time in a cast all over again. As I looked over at my chubby baby sitting in her daddy's arms with legs freely hanging over his knees, I couldn't believe she had only made it two weeks before an MRI revealed that her hip had popped out of socket in the cast, and the cast had to be removed. To make matters worse, not only did the saw cut the cast during the removal, but as the clinical aide pushed a little too hard, the saw broke through the cast and sliced a small portion of Ella's lower leg! To me, the whole ordeal was devastating.

Ella's first cast had been hot pink and had covered her entire body from her armpits down to both ankles. There was a small opening in between her legs for her diaper, but other than that, her only visible skin was on her feet, arms, and head, which meant that we had to start giving shots in her arms.

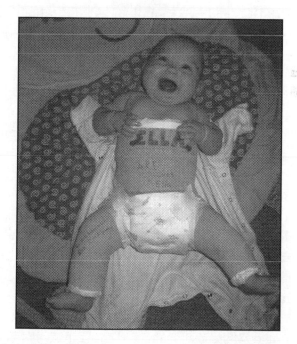

This is Ella while she was in her first full-body cast.

The cast had changed everything about how we cared for Ella. Moving Ella's injections from her legs to her arms had only been one aspect. Another area of change had been the process of keeping her clean. Ella could no longer have baths and required in-depth diaper changing because we layered feminine pads around the opening of the cast, tucked a diaper inside the cast and a larger one that could strap all the way around it. She was a breast-fed baby, so nursing became very awkward, especially since her legs were positioned like she was riding a horse. Not to mention that my now roly-poly seven-month-old was not as small as she used to be and with the added weight of the cast was quite heavy to carry and hold. To have to start the time over and to have lost two weeks of time spent bound in a cast was very frustrating.

As my thoughts returned to the party, God reminded me of a verse that I had recently read, Philippians 4:13, "I can do everything through him who gives me strength." Yes, *that's* what I needed to dwell on. Not, "God, how long must we suffer?" or "Why me?" No. It needed to be, "I can do *everything* through Christ who gives me strength," for I knew living a successful life wasn't just about enduring and making it out alive, but leading others to Jesus and living a full and joy-filled life through Him! And He was there, just waiting for me to accept His help and drink from His bottomless well of grace.

....

As January 2009 was wrapping up, I could not believe all that had changed in the month since my parent's anniversary party. Just a few days after the party, Ella had seen her eye doctor and had been prescribed glasses at the young age of seven months. The tiny, round pink plastic frames that were secured with a strap that wrapped around the back of her head were simply adorable. At that time, Dr. White was able to decipher that Ella's eyes were extremely near-sighted, but did have some vision. She wasn't sure yet about the quality of Ella's sight because the central vision had become distorted when her retinas had partially detached all those months ago, which could not be corrected with lenses. But, in our opinion, some vision was better than no vision. Dr. White also mentioned that Ella most likely had blind spots, but since they had been present early on, Ella's brain would learn to ignore them and would probably never notice that there were empty spots in her sight.

The glasses had been a fun addition to our lives because Ella was able to see so much more than before, and I was given a peek into the will and mind of God when He had chosen not to heal her eyes, for it was those little glasses that sparked conversations about Ella that never would have been started otherwise. We were able to tell the story about how God had taken an impossible situation with my pregnancy and worked an absolute miracle. We don't always understand why or how God decides to answer prayer in certain ways, but I can tell you now, He did work a miracle the day that Ella had her first eye surgery. By allowing her vision to stay hindered, need surgery, and require the use of glasses, God provided not only vision for Ella, but also a way for us to tell her story and share the love of Jesus with everyone whose curiosity was piqued at the sight of a tiny infant with glasses.

Another milestone that had occurred during the month since my parent's anniversary was the second hip surgery. By that point, we were beginning to feel a bit like professionals at taking our child in for surgery, and Ella was becoming well-known around the hospital for her sweet disposition and little pink glasses. The second surgery had been much harder than the first. Dr. Brody asked his colleague Dr. Germowitz to perform the surgery while he assisted because he wanted to make sure that this time the hip would stay in place.

Originally, Dr. Brody had proposed doing a more in-depth surgery that involved cutting and realigning bones, but because of the blood loss that was often associated with that surgery, he opted to repeat the ligament releasing surgery a second time in hopes that this time it would be effective. In an effort to make sure the hip would stay in the correct position, they situated her legs in a much more extreme stance. Ella's legs were in the splits—and by the splits, I don't mean the kind where a person is *trying* to do the splits but just can't get into the position. No, I mean full-on *splits*! They also lined her cast with a fabric rather than the slick, plastic lining used in her first cast, in hopes that it would hold the joint firmly in place. And this cast was purple.

Because Calvin was working, my mom accompanied me for the surgery. I'll never forget how shaken up she was when she caught her first glimpse of Ella after surgery. Ella was experiencing severe pain, not only from the surgery, but from her new extreme position, and my mom just couldn't take it. Her tears flowed freely. I remember being frustrated with her because she was supposed to be there to support me and be strong, but instead she was falling apart and I didn't have that luxury. I *had* to be strong for Ella.

Later, though, when I really thought about it, it had sort of been a peek into the strength that God had equipped me with. More and more, people would fall apart at just hearing about what Ella was going through, and I would realize how God had given me just the amount of strength I needed to get through the day. My mom's reaction had been normal and the same reaction that at times I had held off until later when everyone in the house was sleeping soundly. The fact that God granted me the strength to get through times of my daughter's most excruciating moments was such a blessing, and I knew I needed to be more sympathetic towards my mom.

Everything became ten times harder with *this* cast especially. We were given strict instructions not to allow Ella tummy-time, as it wasn't a good position for Ella's hips. The doctor wanted Ella on her back, which was terrible for her head and the reshaping we were trying to do. Some days I wondered if I'd ever get any housework done in between repositioning Ella's head and trying to keep her entertained. For those of you who have seven-month-old babies, you know what I'm talking about. This is the age when babies want to interact and explore their world. Now, to put a kid in a cast and confine her to one position, whew! It's a tough thing to deal with. Ariana was a great help and often shook rattles for Ella to look at or tickled her under her neck and played peek-a-boo with her. God had definitely equipped our family with the best big sister ever and given Ariana an almost uncanny skill for entertaining her bound-up baby sister.

22

The Call

THE SECOND WEEK IN JANUARY 2009 and two weeks after Ella's second hip surgery, we received an unexpected call from God. While sitting in our Sunday school class listening to a visiting missionary, God spoke to Calvin and me in the same instant. His whisper was as loud as a shout, but because of the absurdity of what He asked us to do, we doubted it.

God asked Calvin and me to sell everything we owned and move to South America to be missionaries in Peru. I know, the sentence itself is absolutely ridiculous when you think about where we were in our lives! But we knew what we had heard, so that very day, we spoke with the director of the missions organization to find out more about the ministry and see what God could have possibly meant by His call. All we knew at that point was that He wanted us to move to South America, long-term, and serve Him.

As you can imagine, prayer coated everything we said, did and thought during this time; not that it hadn't before, but this call on our lives had really turned our world upside down! Ariana was only two years old, and Ella was an infant still fighting the odds of her situation! Not only was she confined to a full-body cast for another three months, but she was still receiving two shots a day of blood thinners to hopefully decrease her chances of the growing clot in her heart causing congestive heart failure or a stroke! What was God thinking when He asked us to move to South America?

And to top it all off, Ella had been having problems with her lungs all winter not only because of her disease, but also because they were so tiny. Any small virus that she contracted resulted in trips to the ER because she couldn't breathe, and she was sometimes admitted to the pediatric unit in the hospital because her condition was so poor. Scary days and long nights of fighting pneumonia were enough to keep us indoors and away from most public events. Even our extended family considered it a privilege to hold Ella as we had to take extreme measures to keep her away from simple colds, because they could result in a life-threatening illness for her! How did God expect us to take this child to a third world country with less than adequate medical care? It didn't make sense, but God seemed to be calling, so we kept on praying, asking Him to open doors and give us confirmations through Ella that this was where He wanted us to go.

Yes, the month of January proved to be an interesting one, and it was not quite over yet.

....

In the middle of January, I had the opportunity to speak at the same retreat that had been held the previous year when my water broke and the young woman, Molly, came to the Lord. As I was wrapping up sharing Ella's story with the teens, I felt the Lord press upon my heart the need to ask the audience if anyone wanted to accept Jesus into their hearts.

"Sometimes it's hard to understand why these things happen," I said, and then paused with the microphone in my right hand and holding the slack of the cord in my left. I looked down at the floor for just a moment and then continued, "And as Christians, we may never know the purpose of our suffering until we're in Heaven, but I tell you the truth, I could have never gone through all of this with Ella without Jesus carrying me!" With the emotion of remembering the ways that Jesus had comforted me in the darkest times, tears threatened to spill over the brims of my eyes. I sniffed and paused, not wanting to try and speak until I was more in control.

After the threat of the tears had mostly passed, I continued with boldness, "If Jesus is knocking on your heart's door right now, I promise that if you open the door, you will never be sorry. I will not guarantee that your problems will be gone; in fact, they may even increase, but Jesus will carry you in His strength and in His provision. He is faithful like we cannot imagine!" With emotion and strength, I went on, "You might think that God doesn't want anything to do with you, that you've been too 'bad' or that you've done something too unforgiveable, but that is not how God works. He tells us in 2 Peter 3:9 that 'He is patient with you, not wanting *anyone* to perish, but *everyone* to come to repentance .'

"When he says that He doesn't want anyone to perish, He really means it. And when He says that He wants everyone to come to repentance, He doesn't mean everyone except you! No! It says, 'He is patient with *you* .' He is not just patient with you when you are a *little* bad or make *little* mistakes. He does not want even *one* person to perish. We serve a God of love and He wants YOU!" Feeling God moving me and speaking through me, I took a deep breath and recited John 3:16, 'For God so loved the world that he gave his one and only Son, that *whoever* believes in him shall not perish, but have eternal life'! When you accept Jesus into your heart and confess your sins, you are a new creation, perfect and clean. In Isaiah (1:18) it says, 'Though your sins are like scarlet, they shall be as white as snow; though they are red as crimson, they shall be like wool'! It does not matter what is in your past, the only thing that matters is that Jesus died for you and if you confess to Him and believe in Him, you will be saved!

"And don't worry about the problems of life. They will come, but in Isaiah 46:4 it says, 'I have made you and I will carry you; I will sustain you and I will rescue you.' He did it for me and I know He will do it for you. Why wouldn't He? I mean, it says right there in Isaiah that He *made* you! Surely if He *made* you, He can also rescue you! And for everyone who believes in Jesus and asks Him into their heart, they become a child of God and an inheritor of all His blessings. In Jeremiah 29:11-13 God makes a promise to us, '"For I know the plans I have for you," declares the Lord, "plans to prosper you and not to harm you, plans to give you hope and a future. Then you will call upon me and come and pray to me, and I will listen to you. You will seek me and find me when you seek me with all your heart."'"

I paused then, for just a moment, squinted my eyes and looked into the audience, trying to see the young faces against the shining spot lights that blared on me. Inhaling and closing my eyes as I felt the love and peace of Jesus in my heart, and hoping that these teens would see the difference He had made in my life, I opened my eyes and finished with feeling, "Jesus loves you *so* much, open your hearts to Him and He will turn you world . . . Up. Side. Down," I emphasized the last three words by pausing in between each one and then added, "In a good way!" With a big smile and a little laugh I was done.

After the youth pastor wrapped things up and gave directions for the nightly activities, two young women individually approached me and said that they were ready to accept Jesus as their Savior! "Do you know how to ask Jesus into your heart?" I asked Sasha, the seventh grader who came to me first.

She glanced at me from under her dark lashes and shook her head "no," so I offered to lead her in prayer. When she accepted, I began praying with her as she repeated my words, "Jesus, I believe in you! And I want a relationship with you. I know I have sinned. Please forgive me and wash away my sin." As we prayed, I hoped that the prayer wasn't just a ritual for Sasha, but a true heart commitment. I continued, "Please fill me with your Holy Spirit and give me new life. I am yours, Jesus. I love you. Amen."

After leading both girls in prayer, each one embraced me in turn for long moments and then hopped on the bus that was taking them back to their cabins. I couldn't help but be amazed at how God had worked that night and how He was using our story to change lives. "Two girls actually accepted Jesus Christ as their Savior tonight!" my mind reeled. "*Two* more lives are going to live eternally because of the impact Ella's story has made on them! Wow!"

Amazing things happened at that retreat, but one bad thing resulted from it as well. Ella picked up salmonella, and for weeks afterward she had terrible diarrhea that absorbed into the fabric of the cast and created an impossible mess and stench for all of those who cared for her. Finally, after three weeks of complete disarray, Ella's cast was changed.

> "The Lord your God is with you, he is mighty to save.
> He will take great delight in you, he will quiet you with
> his love, he will rejoice over you with singing."
>
> ᔍ ZEPHANIAH 3:17

....

After a month and a half of intense prayer and seeking God's will, we felt undeniably pressed to look further into the possibilities of becoming missionaries in Peru. We set up an interview with the board of the organization we were looking into becoming a part of. Going into the interview, we had no idea what to expect or what God had planned, but it was something we were being led to do, and if God closed the door to Peru after the interview, then we'd know it wasn't for us.

For some reason, the missions board accepted us for the job of Cluster Support Parents to a group of young, single missionaries who would be planting churches in Peru. We found it hard to believe that they found us right for the job even though we had two young children, one of whom was battling severe health issues and bound in a full-body cast. We just understood it to be God moving us more in the direction of Peru. Even though it made no sense, we knew that it made sense to God, and so we knocked on the next "door" to see if it opened as well.

When we went to meet with our missions recruiter, we brought both of our girls along— Ella, in her full-body cast, and Ari, into everything as she was at two and a half years old—just to see if would change his mind about us. With what we thought was a total lack of logic, he welcomed us on board and told us that we'd be leaving for Peru in January 2010, only nine months away!

With each opened door, Calvin and I put new "tests" up to see if we were really heading in the direction God wanted. It was so unbelievable to us that God would send us to such an unlikely place considering our situation. One of the tests for us, and a requirement of the organization, was that Ella had to be cleared of all medical ailments and considered well enough for South American life. This seemed like a huge long-shot, so we knew that if a door was going to close on our Peruvian adventure, this would probably be it. Another huge test would be raising the $60,000 needed to become long-term volunteers in a foreign country for two and a half years!

In mid-March 2009, just after Ella's third full-body cast (an orange one) was removed, she received another echo cardiogram on her heart to check on the blood clot that had been growing consistently since they found it almost eight months before. I just knew that this was going to be the kink in the line; if anything would stop us from going to be missionaries (besides the money), it would be a heart condition. Once the doctor began the exam and echo on Ella's heart, I just prayed that the Lord's will would be done in Ella's life and in our lives as a family. Suddenly, interrupting my thoughts, the cardiologist, Dr. Argon, said with surprise, "I don't see it!" Her brows creased as she squinted her eyes in an attempt to better view the monitor in front of her. "It's not here. The clot isn't here."

At once, I had a sickening feeling, because my first thought wasn't that the clot was gone, but that it had detached and was on its way to Ella's brain to cause a stroke. I kept my eyes glued on my daughter who wiggled under the movement of the probe on her chest. "Would God allow her to live all these months only to take her by a stroke now?" my mind worried. I watched intently, waiting to see any signs of a stroke.

"Oh! There it is," Dr. Argon exclaimed. "The clot is there, but it's so tiny you can hardly see it." My heart leapt within my chest, and instantly I felt terrible for thinking the worst when really, we had just been the recipients of another miracle!

"What does this mean?" I asked, almost out of breath from shock. "Well, it means that this will never be an issue for Ella and you don't have to see me anymore. The clot has shrunk so much that it will never be problematic again. Give me those papers, I'll sign off on your move to Peru," she said with a wink.

"What?" my mind screamed. I was happy and shocked all in the same instant. "How can this be?" the human side of my thoughts argued, but my heart knew, God had worked a miracle just because He could. I bet He never gets tired of seeing our surprise every time He does something impossible. You'd think our family would be better at anticipating God's miracles since we'd seen so many, but nope, we're astonished every time. I guess that's why we're human.

Ella's cardiologist had signed off on our move to Peru, but we still needed four other really important doctors to sign off on good health before we could *really* make plans. Signatures and letters of release from Ella's pediatrician, hematologist (blood doctor), ophthalmologist, and orthopedic surgeon were needed before we could move forward, and even though the list was long, we were starting to see God's plan unfolding.

Doubt about our new calling started to decrease and anticipation and excitement grew.

....

Everything seemed to be falling into place, and by mid-April we had "OKs" from every doctor, including the surgeon regarding Ella's hip. Even up until the cast came off, we were unsure if the surgeries had been successful, but after only a few months out of the casts, Ella showed great signs of improvement. Dr. Brody did think that there was a small possibility for another surgery on her left hip, but not for several years, so he signed off on a two-year stay in Peru.

23

Open Doors

IN THE MONTHS FOLLOWING ELLA'S "release" from her full-body cast and from many of her doctor's appointments, her schedule became full with different kinds of appointments: therapies. It was recommended to us that Ella see a developmental therapist who would help her to catch up to where other kids her age were functioning. A physical therapist was also assigned to Ella to help her regain movement in her left hip, and a therapist from the school for the deaf and the blind met with her to help her cope with limited vision. Ella saw each therapist once a week, and luckily they all came to us!

Only one therapist required a thirty-minute commute and extensive daily "homework": Jessie was Ella's therapist who worked with her on swallowing foods and liquids. Once Ella started eating solid food and drinking from a cup, we became aware that Ella had a swallowing disorder. Every time she took a sip, the fluid would reach her throat before she was ready, and it would leave her coughing and gasping for a breath.

The condition was especially alarming because every time fluid would sneak into her lungs, Ella was at a higher risk of contracting the already-familiar illness pneumonia. Until we had done enough therapy to strengthen and train Ella's swallowing muscles, we were forced to thicken all of Ella's drinks to make them more manageable for her. While Ella's swallowing disorder was not an issue that was going to halt our plans to move to Peru, it was one that was unsettling, and it left us doing time-consuming mouth-stimulating therapies to try and resolve it as soon as possible.

Ella's therapist from the school for the deaf and the blind, Jody, did not stay around for long. It only took until Ella spotted Jody's tiny golden necklace for her to realize that Ella could see far better than anyone thought, and Ella was discharged from services. But our developmental therapist, Shelly, stayed on and not only helped Ella learn many important skills, but also became a very close friend to our family. Libby, Ella's physical therapist, was much the same. Her heart for Ella's growth and development moved us and created an instant bond and deep friendship. We will never be able to thank these incredible women enough for the work they did with our girl and the milestones they helped her to reach.

....

Ella's first birthday came on May 8, and with it came immeasurable joy and satisfaction! In only one year, we had gone from fighting for our daughter's life to her miraculous healing and the possibility of a ministry in South America! We were indeed experiencing God's love and fulfillment!

> "And I pray that you, being rooted and established in love,
> may have power, together with all the saints, to grasp how
> wide and long and high and deep is the love of Christ, and
> to know this love that surpasses knowledge—that you may
> be filled to the measure of all the fullness of God."
>
> &❧ EPHESIANS 3:17-19

....

With doors flying open to the ministry in Peru, we continued putting one foot in front of the other in pursuit of God's will. Amazing things happened in order for us to be able to move south, including the highly unlikely sale of our home. To anyone who puts limitations on God or writes things off as impossible, I warn you . . . the God of the Bible is not a God of impossibilities or even possibilities, but *miracles*! Even when it seems that there is a dead end with no way to turn, God opens a secret door and a magical road appears, just as the Scripture reads, "Jesus looked at them and said, 'With man this is impossible, but with God all things are possible'" (Matthew 19:26).

In May 2009, when we first consulted with a realtor to sell our home, he told us that we'd be lucky to sell our house by the time we left in January, which was nine months away. "With the other 20 or so houses in your neighborhood that are for sale, and the bad economy, you might want to consider just renting your house out. We'd be very lucky if your house sold in a year!" he advised.

But God had laid it on our hearts that we were to sell everything. We had not received any information in detail (as is usually the case when you're living for the Lord) as far as what God wanted us to do once our time was up in Peru, but the call was clear and we felt very certain that God wanted us to sell everything.

Knowing that it could take us over a year to sell our home, we did everything necessary to make it ready and get it on the market as soon as possible, including bringing in sod for the backyard and putting up a fence. I believe May 15, 2009, was the day that our home was placed on the Multiple Listings System with photos, and by 5:00 p.m. that evening we had people interested in buying. By the afternoon of the next day we had an offer, and three weeks later we closed the deal and became "homeless."

Selling our possessions was a similar story. I placed ads online with pictures of each item: home décor, furniture, toys. Within a few hours, sometimes a few minutes, I'd get a call that someone wanted to come and pick it up. People would come to buy one thing, and when they found out that everything was for sale, they'd walk into our house and "shop," sometimes leaving with 10 or 15 items! By the time we moved out of our house that had just sold, we had only the bare essentials left.

For the next three months, we lived with Calvin's brother and his wife, Eric and Mindy Wilkins, who kindly put up with two wild kids and less living space. When we were down to the final four months before we were due to hop on the plane, God opened doors like we could not believe, starting with a house that was all our own and required no rent! My cousin, Richard, whose mother had passed away earlier in the year, offered us her home until our departure and refused any rent or utility payment of any kind, so we finished out our last few months in that house.

Next, phone calls rolled in one by one with people who had ideas on how to raise money for our upcoming ministry in Peru. With every fundraising opportunity came countless people ready and willing to help in whatever way they could. We organized and held a walk-a-thon, set up a booth at our church's holiday boutique where ladies of our church donated baked goods and hand-crafted items that were sold to benefit our ministry, held countless yard sales, and spoke at several churches and missionary groups that also donated thousands of dollars so that we could live in Peru and share the love of Jesus with people who had never heard the Good News of Jesus Christ!

One night, I remember lying in bed praying, "God, we still have so much money to raise. If it's your will that we move to Peru, please bring in the money. Put our names on someone's heart tonight with the amount you want them to give to our ministry. We know that you are in control of all the money in the world and if you want us to go, it will happen. Without you, God, this is impossible, but you've opened so many doors already, we know that you want us in South America. Pave the way, Jesus," my heart cried out.

The very next day, I stopped in at a Walgreens while spending some time with my dad. While walking the aisles, I ran into a friend from church, and she proceeded to tell me something that I will never forget, "Jen! It's crazy that I ran into you today! Last night, God laid your family on my heart and told me the amount that we needed to give you for your ministry in Peru. I could not find your donation card anywhere, but God would not release you from my mind, so I looked and looked until I finally found it and sent in the money! God bless you, sweet girl, we love you and are praying for your family!"

Wow. God had worked and put my family on this woman's heart in the exact instant that I had prayed for Him to do that very thing! What an amazing God we serve! How big must He be to answer even our smallest prayers! The amount on the check that she sent in was $2,500, and everyday more and more money came in from people who felt led to support our ministry! Little did I know, that was just the beginning.

....

In the midst of our ever-quickening way of life, Calvin never missed an opportunity to say "I love you." Over the course of the trials we experienced with Ella since before her birth, our relationship had ridden a pretty rough roller coaster. It seemed as if we had been tied up with a weak and flammable rope and thrown into a blazing fire, doomed to separate as soon as the first spark settled on our rope of unity. But instead of coming out blistered and burned, by the power of Jesus Christ, our love for each other was refined by the flames of tribulation. We came out united and purged by the holy fire of God that left no corner of our hearts untouched.

The morning of October 7, 2009 I awoke to find this note on my Bible:

Jennifer, my lovely bride and soul mate!

I want to express to you my deep love for you. Too often I take you for granted, but you are a mighty gift from God. Mighty in the fact that you love Jesus and answer to no other. Mighty for following Him wherever He leads. Mighty and trustworthy for marrying me not knowing where that would lead! What an amazing 5 years it has been.

You don't know how much I depend on you, rely on you, and don't deserve you, yet God has been gracious to me and has given you to me. I have made many mistakes in our marriage but you have forgiven me anyway. I am enjoying growing closer together each day and look forward when we can grow every day together, as we fulfill our pledge that has been commissioned to all believers. (Peru)

As you think of me each day, pray that I will continually seek refuge in Jesus, keeping my thoughts on Him, on you, and on whom I am living for in this day to day struggle.

I want the Lord to tell me "well done, good and faithful servant" when I enter his kingdom. I need to live my life accordingly and need my wife's daily prayers to help me be a man of God. I love you with All my heart!

-A bond servant to Christ,
Your husband Calvin

....

Autumn brought a new set of unexpected circumstances with Ella's health. It seemed as soon as the weather cooled, Ella was hospitalized for croup and released just in time to take a week-long trip to the Oregon coast with Calvin's parents. As well as fighting several other respiratory ailments, Ella scared us again with contracting RSV (respiratory syncytial virus) and needing special breathing treatments only four weeks before we were scheduled to move to Peru. With $40,000 dollars raised and our departure date creeping quickly up on us, we weren't sure what to make of Ella's recent respiratory problems.

We had thought that Ella's health risks were gone. What if she had a problem in Peru? Would they have sufficient medical equipment to treat her? Would we be close enough to modern technology? God soon addressed our immediate concern by healing Ella from her RSV in record time. The doctors told us that it usually took around three weeks for RSV to run its course and for a patient to completely recover. Our fear had been that Ella might have severe breathing issues during our long flights, but God calmed our fears by taking away her RSV and giving her a complete recovery in only two days!

Just to be safe, we contacted the missions organization to make sure that there would be adequate oxygen and medical facilities that could care for Ella in case of an emergency, and they assured us that as long as Ella did not need any in-depth surgeries or testing, the local clinics should be able to treat and diagnose small respiratory issues.

....

On January 24, 2010, Calvin and I spoke at our home church in Nampa, Idaho, sharing about our journey so far with Ella and how God had led us to become missionaries in Peru. When we had finished speaking, Pastor Conrad returned to the stage and began to pray. His prayer went something like this, "Lord, we just don't know how to pray today. We want to help Cal and Jen financially and there are so many ministries that need our support. Already today we've taken our normal offering and an offering to help with the relief efforts in Haiti; help us to know what you want us to do." Without even finishing his prayer, people began trickling to the front of the sanctuary with their monetary gifts of love to our ministry and laying them on the altar.

At first, I wasn't aware of what was going on because my eyes had been closed for the prayer, but when I realized the long silence, I opened my eyes to discover people flooding to the front and laying their monetary gifts on the wooden kneeling bench that lined the front of the sanctuary. Overwhelming feelings of gratitude and humility pulsed through my body, and tears started streaming down my face almost as quickly as people came to the front. We go to a very large church, so this wasn't just three or four people coming to the front with sacrificial offerings to our ministry; it was more like hundreds. Our sanctuary is divided into four large groups of seats, and each of the three separating aisles was filled with people waiting to drop their gifts on the altar before Jesus.

Before that day, $40,000 had already been given and pledged, and part of our presentation had been offering the opportunity to participate in a match program that one of the couples in our church was sponsoring. One of the incredibly huge moments in our journey to Peru had been when this couple approached us and told us that they wanted to donate to our ministry, but wanted to get others involved, and so they offered their donation through a match program: if $10,000 was given by others, that couple would match it with another $10,000! I am not sure what $10,000 means to you, but to us it was an unimaginable amount, and we considered it a gift straight from Jesus.

And now, watching the response of our congregation as they poured out love and offerings, it was more than our nerves and emotions could handle. Tears just continued to roll down my cheeks as the Holy Spirit filled and moved each person in that service. It's a day that neither Cal nor I will ever forget in our entire lives. Over $20,000 was raised that day, not including the $10,000 incentive, so not only were we fully funded for our two and a half years in Peru, but we had excess!

"Ask and it will be given to you; seek and you will find; knock and the door will be opened to you. For everyone who asks receives; he who seeks finds; and to him who knocks, the door will be opened. Which of you, if his son asks for bread, will give him a stone? Or if he asks for a fish, will give him a snake? If you, then, though you are evil, know how to give good gifts to your children, how much more will your Father in heaven give good gifts to those who ask him!"

&❦ MATTHEW 7:7-11

....

With our house and possessions sold, and eight suitcases packed with necessary clothing and toys, we moved our lives to South America to the city of Arequipa, Peru. The first few months were rough as we learned all about living in a different culture and not being able to speak the language. There were days of complete homesickness and dislike of the host culture, but then there were also days of joy and blessing so deep it made up for the hard ones.

We worked very closely with 12 young single missionaries who worked hard to plant churches in our community. Six of them were North American and six were Peruvian. A Peruvian and an American were paired up to be a team, and together they worked to start mini-churches in their assigned areas around the city. Having the Americans was such a wonderful sense of home during those first few months as we were getting used to a foreign place; it was the hardest thing we've ever tried to do. And our Peruvian singles added such an amazing dynamic as well; each one was truly a blessing to get to know.

There were some interesting differences about living in Peru that we had never experienced while living in the States. For instance, in Peru, we couldn't flush our toilet paper, power and water outages occurred frequently, shopping was completely different as we purchased our produce in open-air markets and had to bleach any fruits or veggies before we dared take a bite, and the water was what they called "raw" and needed to be boiled before drinking. There are so many things that differed between Peruvian living and American living, but one that affected us perhaps more than any of the others was living with no hot or even warm water.

**This is Ella with "Maria" and "Carolina", a mother
and daughter we met at the Plaza in Arequipa.**

For two months, we lived in our apartment with absolutely no form
of heated water whatsoever. Calvin showered every other day in the frigid
waterfall that our shower produced, but he was the bravest of us. I showered
every other day, but only washed my hair in the freezing liquid that caused
head aches once a week! Our girls however, were somewhat spoiled. There
were no built in bath-tubs in Arequipa, at least from what we saw, and so
we bought our kids a small bucket in which they could bathe. I'd boil a
pot of water and mix it with the water from the sink which made a nice,
warm bath for my kids to splash around in. After two months of freezing
showers, finally Calvin installed an electric shower head in our bathroom.
They are illegal in the United States, which totally makes sense since it is
a combination of electricity and water to produce heated water, but after
losing about 10 pounds just from shivering, we decided it would be worth
risking electric shock.

24

Peruvian Medicine

THE FAMILIAR BARKING COUGH CAME from the girls' room one night as Calvin and I were sleeping. I immediately recognized it as croup, a respiratory virus that had caused us to take our blue-lipped daughter to the ER several times in the past. I hopped out of bed and ran to see which girl was struggling for air. When I came upon the twin beds lining either wall, I realized it was Ella, and she was wheezing with each breath. I picked her up and brought her into the small room that was just outside her bedroom.

There, I took off her shirt to assess the situation and see if she was retracting (struggling so hard to breathe that the skin starts to be sucked in between the ribs). Her skin pulled deep into the rib cage with every breath, sending an alarm off in my brain and leaving me mentally searching for the proper treatment. Calvin came and held Ella as she cried and labored to breathe while I searched our closets for the inhaler and distribution tube and mask we had brought from home. Finally, after what seemed too long, I found them. Placing the mask over Ella's mouth and nose, I pressed the medication into the inhaler which dispersed it into the tube and mask and delivered it to Ella's mouth and nose.

After only five minutes, Ella started to breathe easier and look more relaxed. This hadn't been the worst case of croup that Calvin and I had ever dealt with, but it certainly had a new feel to it in a foreign country. The ER wasn't just down the road, and we didn't have a car even if it was.

If we had an emergency in the middle of the night, we would have to hail a taxi and drive to the other side of town before finding the nearest medical center. Luckily though, the inhaler worked this time, and Ella seemed to be resting easily. Calvin and I put her back to bed and went back to bed ourselves, though neither of us slept very well, because if this case of croup was anything like what she'd had in the past, this would only be one of several nighttime attacks to come.

Surprisingly, Ella didn't have even one more attack during the night, and the next morning, she played like nothing had ever happened. I wrote it off as a close call and went about my day of laundry and housekeeping, which was an all-day task considering we hung our laundry to dry on the roof and did dishes by hand. About midday, I noticed that Ella's croupy cough had returned. *This* was unusual, because normally Ella only had the cough and wheezing during the night. She had never experienced an outbreak or attack during the day. I watched her closely as she continued to play and noticed that she wasn't wheezing, so I disregarded it and assumed it was just a flare from the night before.

Fifteen minutes later, my tiny two-year-old was lying in my arms, lips bluer than ever before, barely sucking in enough oxygen to stay coherent. As quickly as I could, I gave her another dose from her inhaler, but after precious time had passed with no improvement, I picked up my cell phone and called one of our young, single volunteers and asked him to rush over and help me get the kids to a clinic. Calvin was in town working and too far to get home in time to help, so the single missionaries that were across the street at Bible school were my quickest aid. The first one to arrive was a young 20-year-old boy named Greg. He met us as we were leaving our home and asked me, "What's the plan?" I told him that we needed to find a clinic and oxygen right away.

After getting a glimpse of Ella's deathly gray coloring and ragged breathing, Greg grabbed her from my arms and began running down the half-paved street. As he was running into a small tienda (miniature store) to ask for directions to the nearest medical clinic, some of the single girls ran up to meet me and I asked them to take Ari as I ran after Greg. When I reached the tienda, Greg had already run out the doorway and continued down the street with Ella bouncing in his arms. He yelled to me as he looked over his shoulder that the lady in the tienda told him there was a clinic with oxygen just down the street. I struggled to keep up with his long strides and was glad I had followed him when I did, because by the time I caught up with him, he'd stopped a little pick-up truck to ask for directions, but instead of giving him directions, they just told him to hop on.

So, with my little daughter in one arm, Greg hopped onto the back of this little truck and hung on with the other hand. I barely made it in time to hop onto the other side of the tailgate before the driver took off. We rode for what seemed like five minutes as we bounced down the rugged, pot-holed roads of Arequipa on the back bumper of an old S10 pickup truck. As soon as we arrived, Greg (who was still holding a blue Ella tightly in one arm) jumped off the tailgate and ran inside. I asked the driver if I could pay him, and when he refused, I rushed into the medical clinic. When I got inside, Greg and Ella were nowhere to be seen. The lady at the desk instructed me to go down the hall and pointed me into a small room where I found Greg holding my baby with an oxygen mask over her face and praying ardently that God would save her life.

After three months, my Spanish was still very weak, so I didn't understand much of what was going on, but realized right away that God had sent me the perfect helper because Greg had been in Peru a year longer than we had and spoke pretty fluently with the locals, so he was able to translate for me.

Even with the oxygen and breathing treatment the doctor decided to give Ella, her wheezing persisted and the look of death swept her little body, giving me terrible memories of when she had narrowly escaped death as a newborn. After several minutes they decided to give her an injection of adrenaline to help open her airways.

A breathing treatment, two injections, and one more breathing treatment later, Calvin finally arrived to the small country clinic as Ella was starting to breathe easier and fell fast asleep from her tiring struggle for life.

The country doctor confirmed that the scare had been a case of croup and gave me some medication to take home in case of another attack. With Ella sleeping soundly in my arms and breathing much easier, we were released from the clinic and made our way home on foot.

During our time in Peru, that day when Ella contracted croup and gave us the scare of our lives was by far the most terrifying experience we had! Several other instances of croup had warranted concern, but every other case had been in the safety of the United States. This time, we had seen the amazing provision of Jesus as he sent the exact right person to help me that day, showed us the way to a close medical clinic, and provided the proper treatment all in time to save Ella's life!

Jesus was very close to us during our time in Peru, constantly looking out for our kids, and especially Ella. I cannot count all the many times while Ella was learning to walk that she fell on concrete or tile, since there was hardly any grass or carpet in Arequipa where we lived. One time in particular, Ella fell from a table and landed on her head on the hard cement. Without seeing the fall, I heard her skull hit the surface from twenty feet away and feared that her head was split wide open, but when I got to her, she didn't even have a mark! Over and over, we believe that the angels caught our girl as she struggled more than most kids to walk because of her weak hips and poor eyesight.

> "If you make the Most High your dwelling—even the LORD, who is my refuge—then no harm will befall you, no disaster will come near your tent. For he will command his angels concerning you to guard you in all your ways; they will lift you up in their hands, so that you will not strike your foot against a stone."
>
> ❧ PSALM 91:9-12

....

Six months into our ministry, we took a family trip to Lima, the capital city of Peru, to complete our residency. While we were there, we took advantage of the more advanced medical facilities and had some routine checkups on Ella just to see how her hip and eyes were doing. I was a bit nervous about her eyes because I wasn't sure if the doctor's office would be able to get her new lenses to fit in her frames if needed, but her hips were almost an afterthought since she'd been given the "OK" for several years from her surgeon in the States. After meeting with some of the medical brains of Peru, we found that we should have had our concerns flipped around. The optometrist checked Ella's eyes and issued a new prescription for lenses and assured us that we'd be able to find some lenses that fit in her frames; the orthopedic surgeon, however, found that Ella's hip was much more problematic than we thought and needed surgery, soon.

....

We were beginning to get used to "bumps in the road" of life. Just when we were starting to adapt to life in a third world country, God tells us it's time to pack up and move back home. We had looked into the possibility of having the doctors perform the surgery on Ella's hip in Lima, Peru, but the surgeon refused. The orthopedic surgeon whom we met with in Lima had received his medical training in the United States, but said that he did not feel comfortable operating on Ella in Peru and that we'd have to travel back to the States for the operation.

After we sent pictures of Ella's X-rays to Dr. Brody, her orthopedic surgeon in Boise, Idaho, he said that Ella definitely needed surgery within the next six months and that as it was, her hip was halfway dislocated, so the sooner the surgery was performed, the better. Dr. Brody then went onto describe the in-depth surgery that they would need to perform to correct the problem in Ella's hip: "We'll have to go in and scrape out the socket of the hip in order to allow the ball to sit deeper inside, which is called an open reduction. There is also the possibility that we'll need to cut her femur bone in two and rotate it because the bone looks twisted in the X-rays, but I won't be sure if she needs that until I'm in there operating on it."

With this new news, we had our work cut out for us, or rather, we needed to invest in a kneeling mat because Ella was going to require some intense prayer. We had taken a year to prepare and fund-raise for our life in Peru, and now, we were being told that we had to be back to the States in less than six months! Who would take our spot with such short notice? Where would we live when we went back to the U.S.? We had sold our house and all of our possessions; how would we support ourselves? How would we pay for the surgery? We had insurance through the ministry, but as soon as we were home and not involved with the ministry anymore, it would discontinue. How was God going to work this one out? The questions loomed heavily over us, and we did our best to hand them over to God as quickly as they came.

....

Announcing our resignation to the executive director of the missions organization was very difficult. He had become like family to us and we were not eager to depart from him or our team, but once again, God surprised us. The director of the missions organization asked how much time we needed to be gone for Ella's surgery, and after we informed him that it could be quite lengthy with a week-long hospital stay after the surgery, three months in a full-body cast, and possible physical therapy, he surprised us again by asking if we'd like to leave the possibility open to return after six months of recovery.

"Yes!" Calvin and I both wanted nothing more than to finish out our time in Peru! We were scheduled to fly out of Peru on December 31, 2010 for the surgery. Leaving at that point would have only put us in Peru for a little under a year, so the chance at coming back after six months to finish out the 10 remaining months of our commitment was like music to our ears! It was decided that if Ella had recuperated enough after six months, we'd still have a position in Peru to come back to.

God works in amazing ways. Within just a few short weeks, we had received more answers to our questions and prayers. Already, God had fitted our team with the perfect replacement parents, Lance and Trina Walker, who were a middle-aged couple who had lots of years of experience under their belts in their own lives as they had raised two beautiful daughters and followed Jesus with all their hearts since their twenties. Not only were they perfect for the job, but they had already been living in Arequipa, waiting for God to open doors for them in their ministry. They had originally gone down to Peru as Cluster Support Parents for a different city, but for one reason or another, each single missionary who had been assigned to them had gone back to the States, leaving them available to be the parents of our team. *And* they just so happened to be our close friends and mentors, which made the transition so much easier! So, for the time being, Lance and Trina were given the responsibility of our team, but would get new positions upon our return after the surgery.

Another answer to prayer was when Ella was accepted as a patient at a private hospital for children in Salt Lake City, Utah that performed all services free of charge! We had been corresponding with Ella's orthopedic surgeon in the States and mentioned our financial dilemma to him, and without even missing a beat, he recommended that Ella see a doctor at this private hospital where he just so happened to have done his residency and sent his referral to them right away. Within two weeks, Ella was accepted into their database and was on their calendar for a surgery on January 3, 2011.

With every piece of bad news, we had been blessed with a solution. Every frustrating element became untwisted and we were able to rest in the capable hands of Jesus once again. With the awesome realization that Ella's hip surgery did not mean the end of our ministry in Peru, we looked forward to our time in the States with less apprehension and more excitement!

25

Transition

DECEMBER 2010 CAME WITH VISITORS. My parents were planning to visit us and experience our third-world-country lifestyle in just two short weeks. They'd be in Peru for three weeks, allowing them time to experience quite a bit of Peruvian life, including Christmas and New Year's (Peruvian style), then they'd travel back to the States with us for Ella's surgery when the three weeks came to a close.

The thought of having my parents sitting face to face with us in our living room was very surreal because for so long we'd corresponded with all of our family members by online video or e-mail, but we longed to have them *really* with us. There were so many things I wanted to do with them, the first being to show them around our beautiful city and give them a first-hand look at Peruvian culture . . . but besides having them experience our world, I just couldn't wait to hug them.

Already we had missed several important events at home: the wedding of my sister Megan to a guy that I had never met; nine months later, the birth of their son, Jayce; my baby sister Monica's graduation from high school; and the wedding of my cousin Alyssia to her special man, Ryan. It seems that everyone decided to carry out their really big events the one year we were gone. Even Calvin's brother, Eric, and his wife, Mindy, who had waited years to start a family, got pregnant while we were gone! The list goes on and on of things that we missed out on in the States, so we were excited to enjoy my parents for Christmas and then journey home to celebrate with those we loved, meet our new nephew, Jayce, and be there to welcome Eric and Mindy's little one when he arrived!

....

I always loved watching my girls get settled in on the airplane. They were so excited and seemed to love interacting with the other passengers. As one person after another stepped onboard, my girls would enthusiastically greet them with an "*Hola*" or "Hi" when they walked past their seats. By the end of most of our previous fights, our girls had made several friends. This time, however, was different, almost somber. Ella wasn't aware of the mood, as she was only two and a half and didn't realize that we were leaving for more than a few days, but Ari sat quietly in her seat, staring out the window as she cried. We had just said our goodbyes to our single missionaries who had become just like big siblings to my girls, and Ari, at age four and a half, understood that we were leaving for an extended period of time and would not be able to see them every day.

As the airplane throttled forward and forced our heads backward, pressing against the seats, I closed my eyes and reflected on our time in Peru. Almost one year ago, things had been so foreign when we'd first arrived in Arequipa. The night we arrived, we had been delivered to a part of town that had graffiti plastered all over the small cement shacks that lined the road, which made us believe we were in a very dangerous part of town and had caused us great fear and apprehension, only to find out later that it was one of the nicer areas.

Our time in Peru just wouldn't be the same without several experiences like the one we'd had during our trip to Chile to renew our visas. On the way back to Peru, the driver of our taxi informed us that we were low on gas. "Low" was an understatement. We spent the next hour stopping and restarting, using the fumes that were left in the tank to drive a bit farther. We tried to make light of it and prayed with the kids, but we were seven miles from the nearest town and had two young kids with no water in the middle of the desert. I don't know how many times we stopped and re-started, but I am certain that it was God who got us all the way back to town to coast right into the gas station.

Memories of wonderful times with our team flooded my mind then. Our game nights were a time of fun and bonding. Other times, when we met together and studied the Bible or worshipped in Spanish as a family, had become very special to me. I believed my kids were the luckiest little people in the world because they had 12 young adults who doted on them and loved them up around the clock. I had many memories of the singles giving piggy back rides, building tents, and playing plain old goofy games with my girls. We really had a wonderful life in Peru.

"It's OK, Ari," I heard my mom soothing Ari as she cried for Heather, one of our singles. My mom's words brought my thoughts back to the present. Ari was still crying and looking out the window of the airplane as it lifted off the ground and put the city that had become our home further and further away from us. I was so glad that my parents had taken the opportunity to experience our life in Peru.

At the thought of my parents, a few of the more humorous moments floated into my mind as I remembered things that could have only happened in a foreign country.

One such instance was when we were walking through one of the open air markets with my parents and they were discovering some shocking sights for the first time, like goat heads piled one on top of the other to make a mountain of bloody craniums. Another sight that had become very familiar to Cal and me were the many piles of dead chickens on display, but it was not so normal for my parents.

I think the most memorable moment of my parent's time in Arequipa was when my mom took a shower and experienced an electric showerhead "malfunction." My dad had claimed that our shower had "shocked" him the day before. The next day, my mom was showering when all of a sudden the showerhead burst into flames above her head. Immediately, she turned off the shower and screamed for my dad. After a few moments and a scorched ceiling, the fire went out. It was a good thing that our apartment was made entirely of cement! I jokingly blame the whole incident on my dad, who was messing around with the wires while wet the day before, but in all seriousness, we are so thankful that God protected my mom and no one was injured. It just became a fun story to tell all the family back home during Internet video dates.

Christmas had been different as well. Most of our single missionaries had returned to the States or their homes in Peru during the week of Christmas, but two had stayed behind. Heather, an 18-year-old American gal, and Mitch, another young single American, came over on Christmas Eve to play cards. My parents, the two young singles, and Cal and I stayed up late into the night playing our favorite card game, Ten Nine Eight. We had been told that the Peruvian Christmas starts at midnight with fireworks, so I attempted to stay up, but sleep conquered me an hour early and I was told I missed out on the most spectacular fireworks display that any of our little group had ever seen. Situated on our roof-top, the remaining awake adults gawked at the amazing light display and still talk about what an amazing spectacle it was to see the sky lit up in every direction.

The next morning, we unloaded the socks that we had all hung up above our front window that were filled with Peruvian goodies. Each of us also received one or two little Peruvian trinkets from one another and then we ate some pretty crunchy cinnamon rolls that I had attempted to bake at 8,000 feet elevation. After the few presents were opened and the crunchy cinnamon rolls were eaten, we all relaxed and enjoyed time together for the rest of the day. It will be a sweet memory for years to come.

As our city grew smaller and smaller out the window of the airplane and I tried to remember every detail of the landscape, I realized that I had really come to love Arequipa and the life we had made there. A new chapter in our life was beginning, but it was hard to say "goodbye" to the last one.

....

Six airports, 30 hours, 12 suitcases, and 6 weary travelers later, we arrived in Boise, Idaho to our awaiting family and friends. It was so good to rest in the arms of the people we had missed so terribly the past year. One of best parts for me was watching as everyone checked out my girls. Both of my children had changed so much during the months that we had been gone, so our family had fun inspecting them from top to bottom. Perhaps the biggest changes came from Ella, since she had left the States a year earlier as a bald, crawling baby and had returned a blonde-haired walker.

The day of reunion with our family was bittersweet because we were all so exhausted and knew that in only a matter of hours Cal, Ella, and I would be boarding another airplane that would take us to Salt Lake City for Ella's hip surgery, while Ari would stay in the loving care of our family and friends in Nampa.

....

Our hearts sank as we were thrown a crushing blow in the examining room the day before surgery. Not only did the surgeon, Dr. Melody Wright, confirm Ella's immediate need for a surgery on her left hip and agree that she'd probably need the work done on her leg to untwist it, but she also alarmed us with the question, "Has anyone ever talked with you about Ella's *right* hip?" I looked at her out of the corner of my eye and slowly turned my head to follow my gaze. Calvin and I both answered, but it sounded more like a question, "No?"

Dr. Mel (short for Melody) pursed her lips to the side and delivered terrible news: "Well, her right hip is actually not completely in the socket right now either. There's a chance we'll need to work on that side when we're done with the left. We'll see what we can do for it, though, with the position of the body cast, and hopefully that will be all it needs." As our brains were still trying to sort through the frustrating news, the wind was completely knocked out of us with what Dr. Mel said next. "Also, I'm really concerned about Ella's brain bleed from birth and this little dimple she's got on her lower back. Has anyone ever tested that?" she asked casually.

"Well," I started slowly, trying to remember back to the details of Ella's first few months of life, "Um, they did an ultrasound on Ella's brain to see how the bleed was doing right after she was discharged from the NICU, and I kind of think they did an X-ray or something on her lower back and deemed that the dimple wasn't problematic." "Well, here's what I'm thinking," Dr. Mel began, "With the history of the brain bleed, occasionally even a mild bleed can cause minor cerebral palsy, which causes the hips to fight this surgery that Ella's going to have with a nasty vengeance." I loved the passion Dr. Mel had for her job and her patients. I was drawn to her because she was so down-to-earth and personable. If it weren't for the news she had to deliver, our visit would have been very pleasant.

Having to face not only Ella's left hip needing surgery, but also the chance of her right hip needing work done *and* the possibility of her being diagnosed with cerebral palsy because of her brain bleed, was absolutely devastating. We had been living in Peru like Ella was normal for the last year and now, *now* we were facing the reality of Ella's fragility once again. But that wasn't all Dr. Mel had to say: "And with the dimple, I am concerned that there's a possibility that it's connected to the spinal cord, which would require surgery on Ella's spine if that's the case. I'd like to order a CT scan to check and see how both her brain and her lower back really are when you return in six weeks for the cast change."

I felt the wind go out of my lungs and pure shock gripped me. It was as if someone had sucked the life right out of me and I was left standing there, just an empty shell. Dr. Mel's delivery of the news had been frank and forthright. "So, we came back to the States not only to go through one very in-depth surgery, but also a possible second surgery on her other hip, a possible diagnosis of cerebral palsy, and issues with her spine!" The words screamed from deep within my soul. I felt so vulnerable, so fragile. "How did we escape and feel so normal for our year in Peru when Ella really had all of these issues hiding inside of her? It's like her body's a ticking time bomb, and every time things start to feel 'good,' we should all just run for cover and know that she's about to blow!" Thoughts raged on as I tried desperately to process the information that I had just received about my daughter.

Then, as always, I felt God whisper truths to my soul about our situation, "*Jen, I knew this was going to happen; it's OK, I've got it covered.*" As the words rang through my heart, I knew it was true. God had known all along that Ella had each of these problems and that we'd need to be in the States to care for our girl. He brought us out of Peru so that we could make sure Ella was cared for. He also connected us with an amazing children's hospital that was giving Ella the best possible treatment available for free! Jesus had this under control, which was great news, because I had no control and knew that without Him, I would be absolutely useless.

Cal and I were so thankful for a doctor who looked into every aspect of Ella's health. Dr. Mel seemed to think of every facet of Ella's body and how it would affect her growth and development. As the news settled in that Ella had a few extra issues, Dr. Mel let us in on some details for Ella's upcoming surgery, but one sentence in particular changed our return plans for Peru. It was when Dr. Mel said, "She's going to have a metal plate screwed into her leg bone to hold the two pieces together after it's been sawed apart and rotated, which will have to come out in a matter of nine months." At that, we knew returning to the mission field was out of the question.

26

Surgery

THE LONGEST DAY OF OUR lives was the next day while Ella was in surgery. We were informed that they had extra blood on hand in case a transfusion was needed and that the procedure would take around five hours. For a long time, Calvin and I silently sat on the couches in the lounge. After a while, we made our way to our parent room. We thought about turning on the TV, but it just didn't seem right to zone out and enjoy a program while our baby was being operated on. The hours clicked slowly by, and most of our time was spent praying or twiddling our thumbs as we thought about our precious girl.

After seven long hours, our buzzer went off, alerting us that Ella was out of surgery and would soon be delivered back to her inpatient room. When Ella was finally rolled into her hospital room, I thought I might throw up. She was awake, but she barely looked alive. Instead of a gray color, this time she was a pale green. I had never seen her looking so *sick*. It looked as if something had gone terribly wrong. To top it off, Ella began vomiting. She was crying and saying, "No way! No way!" which was her latest favorite phrase. Calvin and I rushed to her side and tried our best to comfort her. Ella had sported three full-body casts when she was six months old, but somehow, seeing our little two-year-old in the cast she was in now was so much harder.

As Ella gained more and more consciousness and realized that she was bound in a cast, she said the words that I was dreading, "I suk, Mommy!" She was trying to tell me that she was stuck and all I could say in response was, "I know sweetie, I know. I'm so sorry," as I fought back tears. She pushed and grabbed at the cast to try and get it off, "Aw done Mommy," she notified me politely, but I could do nothing to help her. For the first time, I was unable to hold it together and be strong for my little one. The floodwaters of almost three years of medical trials finally hit me, and tears poured forth uncontrollably as sobs shook my body. God had known that I would not be able to handle this surgery alone and sent Calvin to be there and care for both Ella and me. Calvin was so strong and so brave for both of us as he swooped in and held me in one arm and spoke in soothing tones to Ella as he stroked her head with the other. I don't know what I would have done without him.

....

That night was exhausting as nurses and aides came in every two hours to roll Ella from one side to another. Paired with the fact that Ella had an epidural that numbed everything from her waist down was the reality that Ella was too weak from surgery to move her body with the weight of the heavy cast, so the nurses just took the precaution and resituated her body for her. Every time the staff came in to move her, Ella awoke in a fright and screamed uncontrollably. It took her a good half an hour to settle down and go back to sleep every time they came in, only to repeat the whole ordeal in another hour and a half. At one point, Ella was inconsolable until Calvin came in and slept right next to her in her hospital bed.

The next few days were spent weaning Ella off of her epidural and trying to get her to eat. We had realized that it was a big surgery when they told us that they were going to have extra blood on hand, but now that we were experiencing the results, we had a new understanding of how extremely huge Ella's surgery had really been. We had been absorbed with monitoring and soothing Ella around the clock as well as just trying to cope with the pain and frustration she was experiencing, but as soon as she began to get her color back and eat a bit, we regained some sort of awareness and mental capacity to process our own thoughts and questions.

After the first few days of caring for Ella were over, we realized that we hadn't even asked if Ella had required a blood transfusion during surgery. After we curiously voiced the question and learned that they were able to siphon Ella's own blood back into her body and never needed to transfuse any extra blood during the surgery, we praised Jesus over and over!

Another piece of information came kind of by accident when Ella's anesthesiologist came into her room to check on her and asked how she was doing. We responded by saying, "She's doing really well. The first few days have been hard because she wasn't eating anything and in such terrible pain, but now, she's starting to eat and is even starting to sing with me again." A smile curled my lips as I thought of the prayers that were being said for Ella, "You know," I said, "this little gal's got tons of people praying for her." "Well, it's funny that you say that," the anesthesiologist almost laughed, but not because it was funny, almost like she was amazed, then she added, "She's the only case that we've had that has been like railroad tracks," she said as she lined up her index fingers side by side, "That's what we call it when their oxygen and heart rate stay completely stable for the entire surgery. She did absolutely beautifully."

Wow! Our God had done it again! He had pulled our little girl through on such a superior level that it was even evident to the doctors! That news was all my heart needed that day to be completely satisfied.

"The Lord knows how to rescue godly men from trials."

☙ 2 PETER 2:9

....

Five days after Ella's surgery, she was released to go home, which was now my parent's upstairs in Nampa, Idaho. We considered ourselves completely spoiled since the upper level in my parent's house had not only two spare bedrooms, but also a living area that we had all to ourselves and a full bathroom with two sinks! It was almost like having an apartment. After the 50-minute flight home, we arrived with our casted two-year-old; a new, large, bulky car seat that accommodated Ella's casted body; and a wheelchair.

I wish I could tell you that once discharged from the hospital, all of Ella's pain and discomfort was gone, but it wasn't. Night after night Ella screamed and cried because her pain medication would wear off or she was uncomfortable and couldn't reposition herself. I remember one night in particular that the screams came in the form of words as Ella yelled with tears streaming down her chubby cheeks, "Kiss it! Kiss it! Kiss it, Daddy!" Needless to say, Cal and I both ran into Ella's room and "kissed it."

Even with all the pain and frustration, Ella didn't lose her polite disposition. The first day at home, I laid Ella on my parent's carpeted floor and put myself next to her so that I could read her a book. When I was finished reading, I repositioned her on the comfy beanbag that my in-laws had gotten for her and left a stack of books to occupy her attention while I got some housework done. A few minutes later, Ella had flipped through each book and decided it was time to move on, but unable to move herself, instead of screaming and throwing a fit like I probably would have done in her situation, she calmly called me, "Moooommy! Der peeth," as she used her index finger to point "there," even using the word she always said with a lisp, "please"!

I could not believe the patience the Lord had granted our little two-year-old! Only a few weeks before her surgery, Ella had been into *everything*! At our home in Peru, we had to keep the bathroom door shut because a few times I even found her splashing in the toilet! Oftentimes, she'd get into something and make a huge mess, and by the time I'd find it and go to clean it up, she would get into something else and I would have another disaster to clean up when I was finished with the first one! So, for Ella to be so calm and tranquil was an unexpected surprise and an absolute blessing from God. It was as if He'd had a sit-down talk with her about what was going on with her body and she had just shrugged her shoulders and said, "OK."

The peace that Ella possessed wasn't just noticed by her family, but by everyone around her. At church, the ladies in the nursery constantly commented on how happy and content she was just to watch the other kids play while she sat in her wheelchair and fiddled with any random toy. And the other kids loved her! While at the hospital in Salt Lake City, some ladies had come into Ella's room with all sorts of toys for her to play with and offered to glue fabric cutouts of Ella's favorite character onto her new cast just for fun. Dora the Explorer was selected, as it was Ella's most beloved cartoon character, and after she chose several fabric decals, I pasted them into place on her cast. Dora's familiar face attracted all kinds of kids to Ella. She loved showing off not only Dora, but Boots the monkey and Swiper the fox who were also displayed on her hot pink and purple cast.

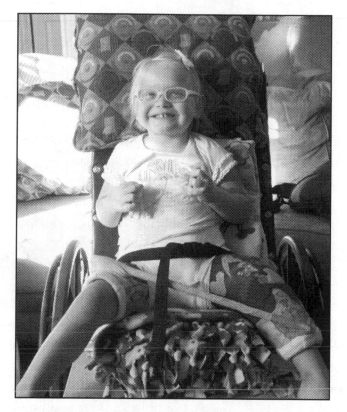

Ella in her full-body cast and wheelchair.

....

After putting off the looming task of giving our resignation to the ministry in Peru, hoping some loophole would be found so that we might be able to return as scheduled, we finally came to terms with the fact that God had closed the door to returning, and we wrote the letter of resignation. Acknowledging the closed door was like slamming a hammer onto our finger; it stung and was a very tender subject for quite some time to follow. But we had to focus on the new direction that God was leading us. The only problem was that we had no idea *where* that was.

Our only certainty at the moment was that we were done in Peru and that Ella still had to endure life in a body cast as well as at least one more surgery (to get the metal plate out of her hip), if not more surgeries on her spine and other hip. We had no idea where we were going or how we'd get there, but we did know that God had led us to this point and we begged Him to keep us close to Jesus and to keep our focus on Him as we followed seemingly blindfolded.

....

In the weeks following Ella's surgery, Calvin hunted tirelessly for a job that could at least provide enough money to purchase the food and fuel we needed every month so that we wouldn't dip into our savings account. From the time he woke up each morning until his head hit the pillow at the end of the day, Calvin searched for a new career. He had hoped to rejoin the local, close-to-home trucking industry, since that was what he had done before we'd gone to the mission field, but no jobs could be found.

After two weeks, a job offer did come, but not the one that Cal was hoping for. A local grocery store where Calvin had applied was very interested in him and called to officially offer him a job with the promise of a "key" position within his first month of work. The offer involved part-time work and low pay, but with no luck at any of the other places he'd applied and not wanting to use too much of our savings, Calvin accepted the job at the grocery store—only until he could regain access into the trucking industry.

With the economy on a continuing downward slide, we were thankful for this new job. It wouldn't allow us to move out of my parent's upstairs loft area, but it would cover our grocery costs and the amount needed for fuel to drive my dad's huge diesel truck that we were using. Because we had originally planned to go back to Peru, all the new realities of staying home started to hit. We realized that it was time to start planting permanent roots, and one way to do that was by buying a family car to save on gas expenses.

The lump in our throats that came from admitting our time in Peru was over was difficult to swallow, and looking for a vehicle to buy was like admitting defeat to our call to the mission field (for the time being), but we knew it was necessary. And so, we searched for what God had for us in the form of a vehicle, and soon found a small SUV that we were able to pay cash for with the money we had saved from the sale of our Honda Civic.

27

Full-Body Cast

As TIME WENT ON, ELLA learned to cope with the fact that she was in a full-body cast. This cast was a bit more liberating than the ones she'd had as a baby because her right leg was partially free. The cast covered her body starting at her armpits and covered her torso and both hips, but only one leg was casted to the ankle. The cast on her right leg ended just above the knee, so we told everyone that passed by when Ella was sitting in her wheelchair to watch out because they were in the "kick zone." Ella practiced movement by kicking her one free leg 24/7!

When we had traveled down to Salt Lake for Ella's first cast change after the first six weeks were over, we were also sent to get the CT scans checking for cerebral palsy and irregularities in her spine done all in one visit. These sorts of scans (MRIs and CT scans) always made me nervous because Ella had to be sedated so that she wouldn't wiggle, but in our experience, the imaging staff had never been able to hit a vein on Ella in order to deliver sedation medication to her bloodstream because her veins were so small and because she was so "healthy," with a little too much meat on her bones that hid the veins from sight.

At one such appointment for an MRI two years earlier, Ella had been poked upwards of *nine* times in an attempt to get an IV started. That day was marked on my mental calendar as the worst day of my life. I had to help hold her down and say, "It's OK," over and over, even though I knew just how bad it hurt to get an IV. The IV was never started and the staff ended up sedating her with an oral medication that only worked because Ella was so exhausted from her hour-long ordeal of being poked and jabbed.

This time, however, after I verbalized my concerns, the medical imaging nurses didn't even attempt to start the IV on Ella; they just brought in the IV team. While the IV team was getting things ready and checking Ella's veins by shining lights through her skin and warming her up, Ariana sang to her and tried to keep her entertained. When the IV was inserted successfully on the first try, Ari rubbed Ella's free arm and sang "Jesus Loves Me" and finished by hugging her little sister tightly. God had definitely blessed my older daughter with the gift of compassion and encouragement!

For once in Ella's young life, we received *good* news. After the CT scan was finished and the results were in, we learned that Ella had absolutely no abnormalities in her spine and that her brain bleed had resolved and was not causing, nor would ever cause, cerebral palsy. She was *finally* "out of the woods"! Good news was as refreshing as I imagined standing under a spring waterfall would be, like balm on our lips, like the smell of the air right after it rains! Yes, this good news was welcome and we were glad to have it!

....

Amid all the amazing learning and growing that Ella was doing, including having an awesome attitude, Satan felt the need to attack our family. One of the ways we felt the extreme attack was when Ella not only came down with croup, but also contracted two different nasty stomach bugs that left her throwing up and having countless bouts of diarrhea each day for about a week the first time and two weeks the second. The first stomach bug hit just as Ella was placed into her second cast. After Ella had recovered from her first stomach illness and completely destroyed her cast with the mess of it, the second bout of the stomach flu came only a few weeks into the third cast, which she was due to wear for five more weeks.

Even with Ella's intense discomfort in her nasty cast, she continued to strive for mobility and displayed an amazing peace. Ella was so bored with sitting activities that, in time, she learned to *crawl* in her cast. After a few weeks of crawling, she advanced to pulling herself up with the help of furniture and then finally, she learned to *walk* a few steps across the room by swinging her hips from one side to the other! I do not know how she did it with the awkward position and legs completely restricted, but she did. It was way more developing than we ever expected her to do while in a full-body cast!

One night we were able to see God carrying our little girl when she woke up crying, "Itchy, itchy, itchy!" Groggy, I half sleep-walked into her room, but when my eyes adjusted to the low light and saw Ella on her bed, my heart broke and I rushed over to hold her. She had been wriggling around on her bed, trying to move her upper body back and forth, with her hand down the top portion of her cast trying to scratch whatever was itching. She was half crying and half calm, saying, "I itchy mommy, I itchy!" After changing her layers of diapers and making sure the inside of her cast was dry, I laid Ella on her tummy over my lap and did my best to rub her back under her cast. Reaching as far as I could into the cast, I massaged Ella's sore body as she moaned and sighed with spurts of relief.

Many times during Ella's back rub, she'd break out in a frenzy and start wiggling uncontrollably and sob, "Itchy, Mommy! Itchy!" For probably 20 minutes, she squirmed and cried out in discomfort. After trying to scratch in every possible place, I just held her, and let my tears come as there was nothing I could do to ease the extreme irritation Ella was experiencing from the unreachable spots in her cast that probably held old diarrhea and grime. But even that night, with unimaginable discomfort, Ella was an amazing example of God's love and grace. Every time I'd rub her back and scratch an itch, Ella would thank me between sobs, "Day du Mama." Feeling helpless, I had said to her more than once, "I'm so sorry you're itchy Ella." And she'd reply in her cries, "Isss OK, Mama." In everything Ella experienced, we could tell that she had a sense that it would not last forever and that Jesus was with her.

....

Ella's stomach bug continued to persist and created many problems. The "messes" that had been caused by the sickness had been so bad that Ella ended up only wearing her third cast for four remaining weeks instead of five. One of the "fun" aspects about Ella's blowouts was that the mess would shoot down both casted legs and up onto her trunk between the cast and her skin, even reaching the top opening and getting diarrhea on her armpits! The stench was unbearable, and we had suspicions that her skin was a bit raw underneath the cast, so a change into a new, fresh cast was definitely in order.

Unable to make the last minute trip to Salt Lake for the cast removal, Calvin stayed home to work, while his mom, Jill Wilkins, accompanied Ari, Ella, and me to the children's hospital where Ella would finally be freed from her casted prison. When the cast finally came off, our hearts broke at the extreme amount of skin damage that had occurred because of the burning liquid that had been stuck next to her skin in the places that I couldn't reach with a wash cloth. Broken blisters and fire-red rashes dotted her torso where the irritation had been the worst. Cal's mom, Jill, watched from the other side of the exam table with her hand over her mouth and tears streaming down her face at the sight of Ella's mutilated skin and miserable cries as the cast was peeled from her body. I stood by Ella's head, holding her hands away from the cast and delicate skin while the nurse got everything out of the way.

During the removal of the cast, Ella's scars from her surgery also made their first appearance. They were both healed so much better than I thought they'd be, with the skin completely fused together. They looked as mended as my C-section scar had looked after a year of healing! The two four-inch scars were on her left side, one off to the side of her abdomen where the doctor had scraped out her hip joint and done the bone grafts, and the other running vertically down her left leg where the doctor had cut her femur bone in two, rotated the bone, and secured it with a metal plate and four screws.

After the cast was safely out of the way, I asked the nurse for a warm wash cloth to wipe Ella's diarrhea- stained skin. While I was gently washing Ella, the nurse went to get the cream prescribed for Ella's rash. After one of the doctors had gotten a glimpse of Ella's blisters and rashes, he had prescribed a cream most frequently used on burn victims. When Ella had been thoroughly wiped down, slathered in the new paste, and dressed in cozy jammies, we made our way back home.

The best part of all had been when I delivered Ella to her daddy's awaiting arms and he lovingly put her into a warm bath. Both the bath and her daddy's arms had been like a healing balm on her skin *and* her spirit. To splash around and enjoy the liberation from her cast for the first time in three months and to feel the warmth and strength of her daddy's embrace had been just what Ella needed. I took in the sight of our young daughter experiencing the freedom to wiggle with no restraints after such a long time of being frozen in the same position. It was liberating and wonderful—a moment I will cherish in the years to come.

....

In the months Ella had been confined to her cast, Calvin had remained diligent in his pursuit of a new career. His job at the grocery store had provided the promised promotion, but the pay had only risen by one dollar an hour, and if we were ever going to be able to move out of my parent's house, a new job was absolutely necessary. A few job opportunities seemed to rise up, only to fall through at the last minute.

We even looked into moving to other states where there was more work, but those doors closed as well. With dead ends everywhere we looked, we began to wonder if we were looking in the right places. Calvin started asking the local Christian university about the possibility of going back to school, and they directed him to our good friend, Heidi, who headed up the "short track" program. After talking with Heidi about the possibility of finishing his schooling, Cal learned that it would take him a little under two years to gain the degree he wanted in business, but without a higher-paying job, we'd be forced to live with my parents for the next two years, and that just wasn't an option. My parents were so compassionate towards us and opened their home so willingly, but we just couldn't put them out for two years!

One good aspect about a bad economy is that homes sell for a lot cheaper! We began looking online at homes in the Nampa area and gained a tremendous amount of optimism at the prospect of being able to buy a home on the income Cal was making at the grocery store! We found small homes that had been build in the 1930s that were selling for $40,000 or less, which would put our monthly payment somewhere around $300! After composing a monthly budget and agreeing that purchasing a home was a real possibility, Cal and I went in to speak with a loan officer at our local credit union.

"To purchase a home with nothing down, you have to have at least a two-year work history," the devastating words came from our loan agent as she shot down our dreams of buying a home anytime in the next two years. "I know you were volunteering this past year and only went two weeks total without any kind of job in the past ten years, but I don't think the lenders will count your volunteer time or the donated money you received as paid income, so you'll have to start your work history over," the agent continued, looking down as she seemed to be searching her brain for some other loophole. After a short moment, she looked up and said, "I'm sorry." With the finality in her voice, we realized that the door had been shut on our dreams to own a home, at least for the next two years. The problem with that was that we could not afford to rent, as the average monthly payment was up around $560, much higher than a mortgage.

In our new-to-us mini SUV, on our way home from the bank, Cal looked at me and said, "You know Jen, maybe God just doesn't want us to put down roots here. Maybe He's got bigger plans for us. I've had a feeling that we'll probably never own a home again, and if He wants us in the mission field, there's a good chance that we won't own a home." With Cal's encouraging words and his loving squeeze of my hand, I knew everything was going to be OK.

God had definitely blessed us in the time that Ella was in her cast, with paychecks every two weeks to cover all of our immediate food and transportation needs. He even provided several checks and anonymous gifts, one that even reached $1,000 that covered Ella's eye exam and new lenses. But the possibility of living on our own was still a ways off in the hazy distance. Now, we just had to make one more trip down to Salt Lake to see what Ella's doctor had to report on the status of her hip, and watch God work out every detail of our future.

....

Our heads spun as we tried to process the news that Ella's orthopedic surgeon, Dr. Mel, was delivering. She had warned us when we had first met with her that Ella could need surgery on her right hip, but at the time, she was hopeful that the hip would adjust while in the full body cast. Now, at the post-op and post-cast appointment, we were learning that although the reconstructed left side looked beautiful, the cast had not helped the right side at all, and Ella would need another very in-depth surgery on that hip, followed by another six weeks in a full body cast. And all of this was due to happen soon, *and* in the heat of summer.

"She *just* learned how to walk again! Now, she's going to have to learn to walk again for the *third* time! How am I going to lift her up when she's even bigger?" Again, questions attacked my heart, "Last time Ella weighed 35 pounds in the cast and it almost broke my back to try and lift her; how am I going to carry her and move her this time?" Thoughts like, "She's going to be so miserable with that heavy thing in the middle of summer," clouded my mind, but when I finally paused long enough to let it soak in, I realized that none of this happened without God knowing it ahead of time. He is never surprised because His power is limitless. Omniscience is among the many credentials of our awesome God, so why was I worrying?

We always prayed that God would lead us and that we'd follow with willing hearts, but does that mean that we'd only follow Him on the easy paths? Are we cocky enough to think that we'd be exempt from the trials? What if *this* is how God will be glorified most, and people will come to know the Lord because of our situation and receive eternal life? "Oh God, make me willing," I prayed earnestly while sitting in that doctor's office as we waited for her to return and go over details for the upcoming surgery. "God, help me to want what you want and to fight the good fight until the very end!"

"How's June 8?" Dr. Mel peeked her head around the corner, into the exam room, eyebrows raised. Closing my eyes, I breathed a silent prayer asking for peace and said, "OK, that'll be fine." With less than two months until the surgery date, my heart sank further, knowing that Ella would miss out on fun times in my parent's boat and in the swimming pool at Cal's parent's place, but even though I was feeling disappointment, I also had a new sense of security in the fact that Jesus Himself was right at our side, helping.

At that moment, I recalled a Bible passage that a speaker at our church had proclaimed a few weeks prior. The verse had caught my attention because of the struggles we were experiencing in our job hunt, and now, it held new purpose as we struggled with trying to make plans for the future as we experienced road block after road block with Ella's health. Proverbs 19:21 says, "Many are the plans in a man's heart, but it is the Lord's purpose that prevails." I knew that what it said was more than true; Calvin and I had been planning up a storm as to what we were going to do with the rest of our lives, but that Bible verse reminded me that we needed to just sit back, strap on our seat belts, throw up our hands (in surrender to Jesus) and enjoy the ride.

"Now to him who is able to do immeasurably more than all
we ask or imagine, according to his power that is at work
within us, to him be glory in the church and in Christ Jesus
throughout all generations, forever and ever! Amen."

ॐ Ephesians 3:20

28

His Grace Is Sufficient

SITTING IN PRESENT TIME (MAY 2011) as I write this book, we are still awaiting Ella's right hip surgery. We have no idea what the outcome will be or what the next obstacles will entail, but if I've learned anything these last few years, it's to wear the armor of God each and every day (Ephesians 6:10-17) and live expectantly for what God has planned. I am positive that being a Christian and loving Jesus did not cause my water to break so that God could show His love. On the contrary, I believe that it was something that would have happened regardless of my spiritual beliefs and that God has used my bad situation for good, to shine His light. I also guarantee you that if I had not had the saving grace of Jesus Christ in my life, Ella would not be here, and chances are, I would not be either.

I have been trying to describe what it has been like to experience God throughout this incredible journey. The only thing I can compare His constant presence and love with is a water supply that never runs out. At times I would get so overwhelmed by thirst for His life-saving grace and forget that all I had to do was lift the bottle of His love to my lips and drink my fill. In the dry times, the water supply never left me or ran out, I just forgot to take a drink. It was not until I died to my worldly way of thinking that I really began to live!

"I have been crucified with Christ and I no longer live, but
Christ lives in me. The life I live in the body, I live by faith in
the Son of God, who loved me and gave himself for me."

&❧ GALATIANS 2:20

Right now, with no clear direction as to where God wants us, we are just focusing on the blessings that God has given us. This past weekend, we celebrated Ella's third birthday and were able to enjoy sweet moments with our child who was at one time doomed to die. Last week, she sat at the dinner table and said, "Yook! I take deep bwefs!" as she inhaled deeply and exhaled slowly. What a miracle! Those lungs were never supposed to exist according to the doctors! One of Ella's favorite phrases that we just love to hear from her little mouth is, "Wet me see hew," as she brings her thumb and index finger to her chin like she's stroking a long beard and thinking hard. But of all of Ella's little phrases, my favorite is when she says, "I wuv you Mommy!" It just melts my heart. This precious little girl was no accident; rather, she was an intricately planned life with much purpose!

How can we be frustrated with the situation that we're in with a miracle like Ella reminding us of God's love each second of every day? There are days when we are weary of waiting and desire a place of our own, a job that can give us material things, or even a purpose and direction for our lives, but if we had those things, would we cling as tightly to Jesus? A verse was recently brought to my attention that has defined this period of my life. In Hosea 2:14, talking about the Israelites, God says, "Therefore I am now going to allure her; I will lead her into the desert and speak tenderly to her."

We are not in the desert because God has forgotten us, but because He wants to tend to us with no distractions, He wants us to hold still long enough that He can rub healing ointment on our wounds. He is preparing us for the rest of our lives, so that He can give us direction and purpose, and when it comes, we'll be ready! Calvin and I have committed to seeking Jesus with our whole hearts during this time of waiting so that God can take this pile of mud (our lives) and mold us into the people He wants us to be. I believe we will be a beautiful masterpiece when He's finished.

Ariana and Ella on July 31, 2011.

As I look back and see the ways that God has already used our weaknesses, I am humbled at the amazing fruits of His glory. One such memory that comes to mind is when we were in Salt Lake during one of our visits, sitting in Ella's hospital room with another family whose son had been admitted and was waiting to be prepped for surgery. One of the nurses arrived and seeing Ella said, "Oh! Our miracle baby is back!" Feeling bad for the other family that had just overheard and not received a compliment on their child, I said, "Every baby is a miracle," and thought that I had solved the brief incident, when the nurse retorted boldly, "No, not every baby is a miracle like Ella. She is *the* miracle baby. I've seen her file," she finished with a wink.

At that moment, I was slapped with the reality of how amazing Ella's life really was. At the children's hospital we saw kids missing legs and arms. Other kids had metal contraptions screwed into their heads that helped straighten their spines, and others couldn't even walk or talk because of their extreme condition! For the nurse to acknowledge Ella's life as miraculous in spite of all the tough cases she'd dealt with was an absolute confirmation that Ella's existence was, indeed, extraordinary!

Another moment of realization came this spring when a good friend of mine, Emily, had come to me and shared how our story had impacted her life. Around the time that Ella was going through her first series of full-body casts and daily shots for the clot in her heart, I had been mentoring Emily. As a blossoming young woman, she had come through so much and had given so much to Jesus that by the time we spoke in church about how God had saved Ella's life and paved the way to Peru, God spoke to Emily and called her to the mission field. The moment had been so special to her that Emily tattooed the date that we spoke in church on her leg. I don't know what you think or how you feel about tattoos, but it was impressive to me that God used our situation so strongly in the life of Emily that she tattooed it onto her body!

Another man testified just a few days ago in church, not knowing that we were sitting in the congregation and said something like this, "This is the kind of church that I've been longing for. The kind of church where God says 'move' and people move! It's like that young couple that had the baby in a full-body cast and had all sorts of other problems, but God told them to go to the mission field and they said, 'OK God' and went! That's what I want and I'm so thankful to be a part of this church."

Wow, who knew we served such a big God—that things we did in the past that we thought were small, were actually life-changing for others? How many more choices or actions have made impacts that we don't even know about? Our goal now is just to drink in the presence of Jesus and ooze out His love on every person we come in contact with. "What if you are never able to afford a home of your own?" you might ask. Well then, I'll know my treasure is in Heaven! Luke 12:33 promises "a treasure in heaven that will not be exhausted, where no thief comes near and no moth destroys." The other day, I passed a less-than-desirable-looking car that had a bumper sticker on it that read, "Don't let the car fool you, my treasure's in Heaven." I loved that!

....

So, what's our family going to do now? Well, we'll go to Salt Lake, have Ella operated on again and be absolutely covered in peace and blessing as Jesus Christ, the Son of God, walks with us and carries us through the really hard stuff. My motto through this time in our lives has been, "I sure hope I don't ever miss the miracles in my life and mistake them for trial." For each trial is laced with opportunity! I think sometimes God moves mountains and we are so inconvenienced by the "move" that we miss the fact that a *mountain* has just been *moved*!

I have a pretty good guess that Ella's right hip surgery is not the end of her life's struggle. Just the other day, we went to an appointment for her eyes, where Dr. White stated that she wasn't sure why Ella's eyes were regressing so much and that it wasn't normal even for other children with the same disease to experience such setbacks in their vision . . . but what are we to do? We can't despair, for we serve a God who has opened unseen doors and paved new paths at just the right time all of Ella's life! And I know that if you asked Ella about her life in 20 years from now, she'd just smile and say, "I'm glad my parents chose life!"

I might be afraid if opposition did *not* arise! With these trials, I consider it a compliment that Satan sees us as a threat! What an honor it has been to be used by God in this amazing journey! I hope that He will never be done with us and that we will serve him with our whole hearts until the day that we die. Yes, there are some days when we get tired and weary, but I know that we will make it to the very last day because I serve a God whose grace and love is limitless, whose strength can sustain me forever and ever!

"But rejoice that you participate in the sufferings of Christ,
so that you may be overjoyed when his glory is revealed."

⁂ 1 Peter 4:13

". . . how wide and long and high and deep is the love of Christ,
and to know this love that surpasses knowledge—that you
may be filled to the measure of all the fullness of God."

⁂ Ephesians 3:18-19

Some people might read this book and think, "Where's the victory? This family is still facing really big obstacles, it seems more like defeat to me." But my perspective is somewhat different. I think this story is all about answered prayer. If you remember back to the preface, I wrote that I think the whole reason for being on this earth after you've received Christ into your heart is to lead others to Him. And just before my water broke, I'd been praying that I'd have an opportunity to share Jesus with others, even as a stay-at-home-mom. Well, sometimes God answers our prayers differently than we had expected, and even though my answered prayer came with much pain and trial, God used it all in bigger ways than I could have ever imagined, and I would not change a second of it. No matter what punches are thrown our way, our prayer is that we'll keep our eyes on Jesus and put one foot in front of the other and continue walking in His hope and amazing grace all the days of our lives! How amazing that it is in our greatest trials and in the midst of the deepest floodwaters of our lives that God uses us, molds us, purifies us, and blesses our socks off!

Jesus says, "'My grace is sufficient for you, for my power is made perfect in weakness.' Therefore I will boast all the more gladly about my weaknesses, so that Christ's power may rest on me. That is why, for Christ's sake, I delight in weaknesses, in insults, in hardships, in persecutions, in difficulties. For when I am weak, then I am strong" (2 Corinthians 12:9-10).

Epilogue

What I want for readers to get out of this book is that we have a God who cares about every detail of our lives and wants to show you the never-ending extent of His love! He wants to use each day and each moment to shape us into God-loving creatures and bring others to His glory, but He is also a God who will not overtake our lives and control us. He is a gentleman, so He will allow us to do things on our own and in our own way. Even when He sees that our attempts will end in vain, He will not push us out of the way and do it for us uninvited. I know that there is fear in letting go of our lives, but hopefully reading this book, and realizing *who* God is and *how much* He loves you, will bring an absolute freedom to let go and fall into His very capable arms.

This is a God of absolute miracles! His tendency for those who love Him is to turn their trials into joys and carve masterpieces out of roadblocks. This God sees a divine solution to every problem and is absolutely invincible! With a life completely surrendered to Jesus, the possibilities are limitless!

It's important for you, the reader, to know that I originally started out writing this book for my family. I felt a burning motivation to get it into ink before the details evaporated from my mind, but as I wrote and the story began to unfold, I realized that it was not only for us, but for countless others, for you. God poured His passion into my soul and revealed that the book would be used for His glory and His purpose, so as I wrote, I prayed, and as I prayed, I wondered, "What is God going to do with this book?" The answer that God kept whispering to my heart is, "It's going to be *big*."

What is *big*? I mean, the word "big" is pretty subjective. Something *big,* in comparison with an ant, could be a rock! Or if you compare it with a tree, "big" could be a mountain, and on a grander scale, the word "big" could represent the universe in comparison with the earth. So, what did God mean, when He said that He was going to do *big* things with this book? I've decided that it really doesn't matter. I trust Him; I mean, He *is* God after all! I believe that He is divinely orchestrating each piece of my puzzle of life, and I am trusting that if He says it's going to be *big,* then it will be *big.*

Part of this great revelation is that God does not look at importance in the same way we do. We look at it as something we've accomplished or a title we've earned or even something on the agenda that takes first priority. That is importance to us. But to Jesus, the only important thing is that we commit our lives to Him and bask in His marvelous presence for all of eternity. So, I've come to the conclusion that if this book touches one life and brings about a life-change and an intimate relationship with Christ, then *that* is *big*! This book doesn't have to be a number one best seller to be important or successful. If one person is saved from eternal damnation and brought to the safety and love of Jesus Christ, then that is bigger than any earthly success could ever be! My hope and goal is that God's love would reach beyond my infantile words in this book and love on you like you've never been loved before!

Afterword

In God's Time...

Only two months after finishing the final draft of this book, God answered our prayers regarding a home and finances. My brother, Josh Miller, decided it was time to upgrade to a newer home and provided us with the opportunity to assume his very, *very* low mortgage. Around the same time that the house became available, Cal's old trucking company called and offered him a full-time position to drive locally distributing food with all of his old benefits, seniority and pay! Blessed be the Name of the Lord!

> Yet the Lord longs to be gracious to you; He rises
> to show you compassion. For the Lord is a God of
> justice. *Blessed are all who wait for him!"*
>
> ஜ ISAIAH 30:18

> ". . . I will never leave you nor forsake you."
>
> ஜ JOSHUA 1:5

References

1. Carrie Underwood's "Jesus, Take the Wheel" is from her 2005 CD *Some Hearts*

2. Gifford, Chris. **Dora the Explorer,** an American animated television series, 2000

3. Kendrick, Alex. **Facing the Giants,** Sherwood Pictures, Georgia, USA 2006

4. **The NIV Study Bible,** ZondervanPublishingHouse 1995

5. **The Youth Bible (NCV),** Word Publishing 1991

6. Vischer, Phil. **Veggie Tales** USA, Big Idea Entertainment, December 1993, an American series of children's computer animated film featuring anthropomorphic vegetables in stories conveying moral themes based on Christianity